An ERP Perspective on Conglomerates and Transborder Corporations Business Process Management, Mergers and Acquisitions

'SAP' is a trademark of SAP Aktiengesellschaft, Systems, Applications and Products in Data Processing, Neurottstrasse 16, 69190 Walldorf, Germany. The author and publisher gratefully acknowledges SAP's kind permission to use its trademark in this publication.

SAP AG is not the publisher of this book and is not responsible for it under any aspect of press law.

Print Edition ISBN: **978-1-78281-091-9**

G2 Rights Ltd, 7-8 Whiffens Farm, Clement street, Hextable, Kent BR8 7PQ

An ERP Perspective on Conglomerates and Transborder Corporations Business Process Management, Mergers and Acquisitions

Day one instructions for SAP R/3 Consultants (SAP R/3 Sales and Distribution, Plant Maintenance and Customer Service, Materials Management, Supply Chain Management, Industry Solution-Oil and Gas, IS-Retail, Shipping, Transport, Logistics, Report Consultants), SAP R/3 Project Managers, Conglomerate and Transborder Business Development Executives and Specialists, Mergers and Acquisition Specialists, Corporate Financiers, M&A Lawyers and Advisers.

Contents

Diagrams

Systems Applications and the Conglomerates - The challenges to seamless business process information technology for medium to large scale Conglomerates and Transborder Corporations

From the very beginning, history of System Applications, from the usage of the *Abacus* centuries ago to the development of binary and programming, suggest scientific and analytic methodology, breaking down of mathematical co-efficients and attention to detail, now applied to business engineering, is an attribute. This is important for conglomerates and transborder corporations to capture every detail of their business processes, logistics and profitability in a much more competitive global economy.

History of conglomerates suggest in the beginning family businesses striving for *Economies of Scale* (as extrapolated by Adam Smith in his magnum opus *The Wealth of Nations (1776)*) in various sectors and businesses, and pushing the boundaries of *Production Possibility Frontiers* both in societies and across industries (as extrapolated by late Paul Anthony Samuelson (1915 – 2009)). Most of these family businesses such as A.P. Moller Maersk, Merck, Philips, Shell, Siemens, Sanyo, Ericsson are now public quoted companies, and beginning from the 1980s got much bigger and urgently required enterprise wide resource planning business system applications (for operational control and global integration) that could capture every detail specially provided by computing and computers. In this new era, for example, Financial Accounting and Controlling (without computing and computers) which used to be the centre of the universe of those businesses were no longer adequate without sophisticated calculations, computing and computers (integrated within the content and capabilities of financial accounting and controlling) to perform this important function.

Companies like SAP AG, Baan, Peoplesoft, JP Edward and IBM were well positioned in the market to provide the required software because they had foreseen these requirements in the late 1960s and early 1970s. They already provided services to the conglomerates and transborder corporations, and recognised the future needs of these conglomerates and the possible computing requirements as a lot of Mergers and Acquisitions (M&A) as growth strategy were taking place and business synergy was required from the perspective of how these businesses would work together to achieve economies of scale. IT applications (including ERP) would play a part in these for those with insight and foresight in their due diligence.

SAP R/3 (Systems Applications Programming) was formed in the early 1970s by ex-IBM employees and the rest is history. It is almost impossible to separate IT applications from the core of activities of conglomerates and transborder corporations, and an SAP R/3 would be the primary business process system and many other secondary systems would be integrated with it to provide a seamless business integration, accountability and the necessary competitive edge.

But there was a unique IT resource problem. Coming out of the recession of the late 1980s, particularly from about 1988, I noticed there was an important organisational shift in most conglomerates and transborder businesses, in terms of the employee skill sets they required. They needed to be streamlined, bigger, sharper, smarter and more profitable in the way they did business. There was a shortage of Information Technology resources and those who graduated from college between 1988 and 1998 (who graduated with other career ideas and ambitions!) were now trusted in a business environment that required Information Technology experts; the levels of this requirement was unthought-of, or perhaps unprepared for, by a lot of schools and universities at the time. IT roles, usually backroom jobs, were now going to come to the forefront. I graduated in this period and it required a change of career plans, and it took a long time to recognise what was actually happening in the employment market. For me it was by accident and destiny's call. It appears, today, that this shortage of skill has been overcome and more experienced staff are now available. Conglomerates and transborder corporations are much clearer on how they want to build and use their IT applications, particularly SAP R/3 and other integrated softwares. IT applications are now becoming the centre of the universe for these conglomerates and transborder corporations, and will one day begin to provide top notch CFOs, Executive Directors, CEOs and Executive Chairpersons because these are the people who actually know how the various businesses, products and sites come together from the ground up.

Today and in the future, the challenges to seamless business process information technology for medium to large scale conglomerates and transborder corporations will be partly due to how to quickly recognise differences of businesses and business systems, how best to achieve business synergy in the shortest possible time (particularly when M&A are involved) and achieve efficiency and profitability.

In a nutshell, in this book I have addressed: (i) A summarized history and complexities of the Conglomerates and Transborder Corporations, for example, different areas of the business - Finance, Sales and Distribution, Production Planning, Customer Service and Plant Maintenance, Reporting etc. - disintegrated (ii) Solutions to resolve the complexities and the integration of the various areas of business, for example, Finance, Sales and Distribution, Production Planning, Customer Service and Plant Maintenance, Oil and Gas-Industry Solution, Reporting (SAP R/3 and Business Warehouse) and other modules on a single platform using SAP R/3 (iii) Integration of IT System Synergy within Deal-making and Mergers and Acquisitions, for example, what lawyers and financiers should know plus a checklist for evaluation and synergy from an information technology perspective.

Introduction: The need for day one instructions and a window into SAP R/3 Seamless Business Process Information Technology

This book, using the sales and distribution module as a case study, is useful for all SAP R/3 functional and technical consultants in the early stage of their career. The same design, configuration and SAP R/3 technical methodology that applies to the Sales and Distribution module also applies to other SAP R/3 modules. SAP R/3 methodology is a systematically organized, top down, step-by-step methodology using the ABAP programming language.

The objective of this book is for you to be able to survive your first days at an SAP R/3 project environment and workplace, particularly if you are switching career or are just green to Information Technology. I hope this book is helpful and succinct, so that you do not suffer information and knowledge overload. Hopefully you should be able to build on this information and knowledge, and thereafter move on to expertise and excellence in your career. If so, the objective of this short synopsis of SAP R/3 has been achieved.

The 1990s were the golden years of the systematic amalgamation of information technology and business organisational processes end-to-end, particularly in international businesses and big major businesses and their end-to-end business processes and scenarios. I am interested in business conglomerates and global corporations and the smooth synergy of different business processes to compete, achieve a coherent whole with knowledge and profitability. With great gratitude to all my former employers and without any specific reference to any employer in this book, I have worked for IBM and Accenture on several global projects, A.P. Moller Maersk A/S, Merck Group, Philips Health Care, Shell, Siemens, SAP, Sanyo, Jungheinrich, Atlas Copco, Ericsson, Nigeria National Petroleum Corporation (NNPC), Reliance Petroleum Business and have travelled and worked in different parts of the world, including the USA, UK, Germany, The Netherlands, Sweden, Norway, Denmark, Australia, Ireland, France, India and Nigeria. I feel very grateful to all for a privileged and jet-set lifestyle. This book is my little way of saying thank you, giving back something to the SAP R/3 community and helping those new professionals coming from behind (particularly those with a career switch to information technology), that will shape the solution architecture, configuration, process designs and development features of the SAP R/3 community in future years, beyond what we know today.

Although with a strong unrelated and higher academic background, I started in an SAP R/3 environment in the late 1990s by accident without any formal or academic knowledge of Information Technology and computers, apart from general usage of computers for general work purposes. I had to survive through hard work, perseverance and willingness to learn. There is always logic in learning any area of knowledge, and SAP R/3 is no different. Progress and success are never achieved through organised disorder, but through hard work, determination, clarity of purpose, and the ability to think research and find solutions to business process problems. SAP R/3 configuration steps, process steps and technical steps are well defined, logical and systematically organized. Even though coming from an unrelated academic background, I understood this very clearly about SAP R/3 in my early years as a consultant, but I never translated this into personal confidence until much later. SAP R/3 requires systematic analysing and finding out the extent of what is already available within the system. Transaction codes and programming are more useful to experts who already know their way around the system, and also know the enhancement and development capabilities of an SAP R/3 system.

On day one, only in exceptional cases will I advise the usage of transaction codes (or short cuts) for beginners. Although we will make an exception in cases where relevant. A beginner must learn to understand SAP R/3 business processes and their application to the end client business organisation. As a beginner in the 1990s, I always wondered, "why don't you explain to me the logic behind the SAP R/3 business system?" or "why don't you use the standard menu path to get to a desired screen instead of dumping transaction codes on me?" And also, "why am I using this transaction code when I don't understand the processes?" or "why don't we use a standard report in the system instead of designing a new one?" I was basically frustrated in my early days without showing it!

It is the intention of this book to spare any beginner any unnecessary learning ordeal and pain, and quickly build the beginner's confidence around the system, and how an SAP R/3 is used by conglomerates and transborder corporations. Nothing is difficult to learn once you understand the logic and you are willing to put in the time, endurance and hard work. While it is true there are many ways to get an answer or learn an SAP R/3 and a lot is possible using the system, as a beginner all you need to remember and know is that whatever you do with an SAP R/3 system there is a systematic logic, clarity and order to it, even when you use transaction codes and ABAP programming logic to resolve a process problem. If you can get that message at the beginning of your career and stay focussed on it, the probability of making a success of your career, yourself and various projects you will work on are much higher.

You should also be a thinker, whether you are a functional consultant or developer. Serious thinking is what you must do when designing solutions for complex organisations, and also note that every project is different.

You are about to learn many years experience in a few hours. Enjoy SAP R/3, the mother of global enterprise business process planning!

For detailed understanding of how to customize and develop an SAP R/3, register for an appropriate training course with www.sap.com

Lionel Etan-Adollo,
Certified SAP R/3 Consultant
Certified Project Management Professional
PhD MTh (Oxon) MA BSc (Econs.) FICS PMP
PhD Oil and Gas Law, Policy and Management
Lioneletan_adollo@yahoo.co.uk
July 2014

Chapter One: Getting started with an SAP R/3 system

I.1 How to logon to the system

In all global corporations that are well organized with well-structured procedures, the System Administrator and his department are the gatekeepers of an SAP R/3 system. Therefore, on your first day the System's Administrator gives you instructions and guidelines on your user identification (logon), your menu set up and will most probably ask you to sign a confidentiality agreement concerning the use of the system and usage of information therein.

Assuming you are starting on an SAP R/3 project with global corporation LEA Group, the System Administrator installs or gives you instructions on how to access an SAP R/3 system on your personal computer or laptop and also gives you your user identification (username and password). Passwords initially provided are changeable.

Once an SAP R/3 is installed, you get started by logging onto the system (*logon*). Fig I.I shows the systems within an SAP R/3 system and Fig I.II shows the various layers of sub-systems, called clients, within an SAP R/3 system. The systems in Figure I.I will usually include the development system (which has a sub-system called the sandbox, which usually does not have much data in it and serves as a play system). In Figure I.I, we show the sandbox, usually a 'play' system; the development system; the quality system (where we test for new configurations and business process testing by the business), and the production system (where real time business operations are done).

Figure I.I SAP Logon

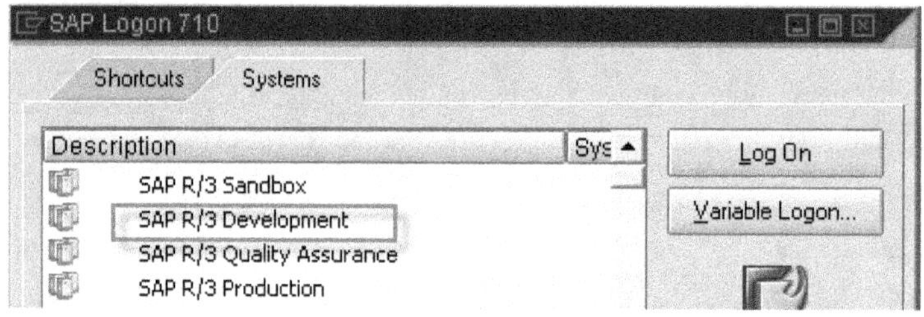

In Fig I.II, you logon onto the development system client 220 and other variations too.

The username created by the system administrator in this case is "EXTLIET".

Figure I.II Entering Specific SAP Client and User Identification

I.II User menu

In the SAP Easy Access screen, as a beginner you can set up your specific favourites and user requirements as you want it displayed in the general work through the opening menu path. The user authorization personnel (System Administrator) can also assign specific role(s) to yourself, meaning only menu paths specific to your role(s) are available for your usage and possible changes, either as a configuration specialist or process specialist. You will have the opportunity to set up your favourites within the context of the authorization given to you by the System Administrator's user assigned role and defined menu for your usage.

For example, the System Administrator sets up the 'User menu for Lionel Etan-Adollo' (see Figure I.III).

*Figure I.III Specific User Menu set up for Lionel Etan-Adollo **by Systems Administrator***

If you drill down the 'User menu for Lionel Etan-Adollo', these are some of the already defined specific user functions defined for Lionel Etan-Adollo by the System Administrator.

Figure I.IV Drill down specific User Menu set up for Lionel Etan-Adollo

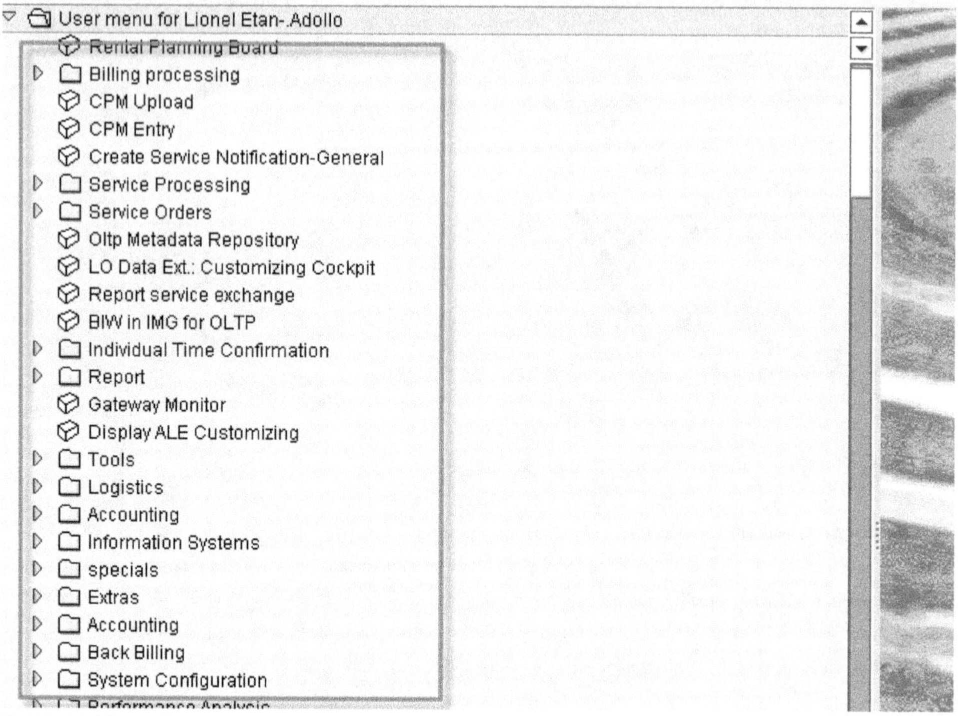

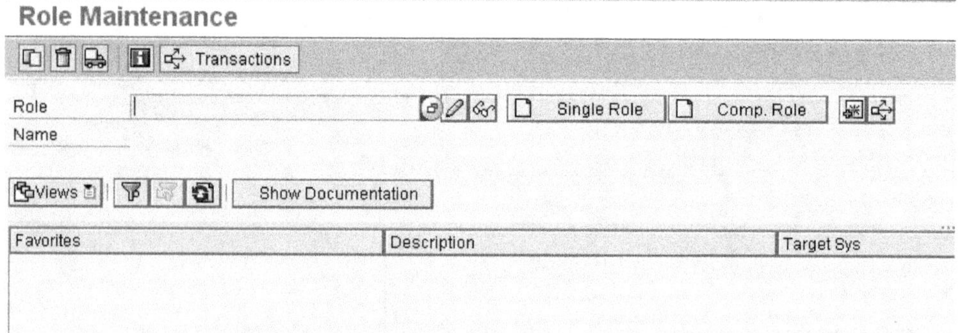

By clicking on [Create role] (*Figure I.V*) the System Administrator is able to define the extent of access and authorization you or Lionel Etan-Adollo has in the system.

Figure I.VI   Role Maintenance by the System Administrator

Role Maintenance

I.III Creating your own user defined parameters

Although this book is biased against usage of transaction codes by beginners, we would make an exception in some cases (See *Figure I.VII **Using transaction codes in** the SAP Easy Access or any an SAP R/3 screen*). By entering user transaction code **SU01** (in the transaction code box 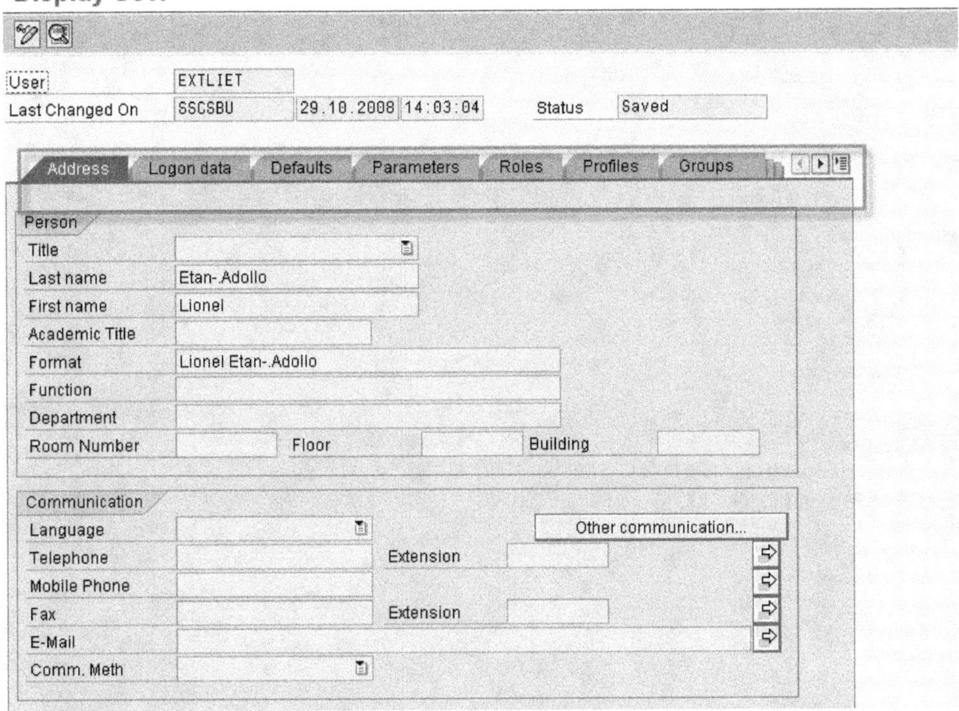 (*Fig I. VII*)) in the SAP screen tool bar and clicking on the green mark symbol (*Fig. I.VIII*) on the left of the transaction code box (that is press the **Enter/Return** key) you can define your user parameters in the various tabs in Figure I.IX.

Figure I.IX User Parameter Definition

I.IV Working through the Menu path

Furthermore, working through the menu path, SAP R/3 configuration steps, process steps and technical steps are well defined, logical and systematically organized. For example, in Figure I.X, under the logistic menu, we have the Sales and Distribution module as a subset and progressively as we drill into the module we continually work through a path well defined, logical and a systematically organized processes. At the core of the Sale and Distribution module is the core data (*master data*) set up specific to the module, and which could also be set up centrally (for the entire an SAP R/3 system process set up, which is generally made up of core modules such as Financial Accounting and Controlling, Materials Management, Production Planning). Master data set up relating to SD will require setting up customer information such as main address (*sold to party*), delivery address (*ship to party*), billing address (*bill to party*), sales order types, the organisational data (*Sales Organisation, Distribution Channel, Division, Sales Office, Sales Group*).

As we drill further down the SD menu path, we see the Sales Support (Inquiry, Quotation and Sales). Further down the path, as we drill further into Sales we have the three core areas: order taking screen; the delivery process (Scheduling Agreement); and the billing process.

Figure I.X User Menu defined for the User

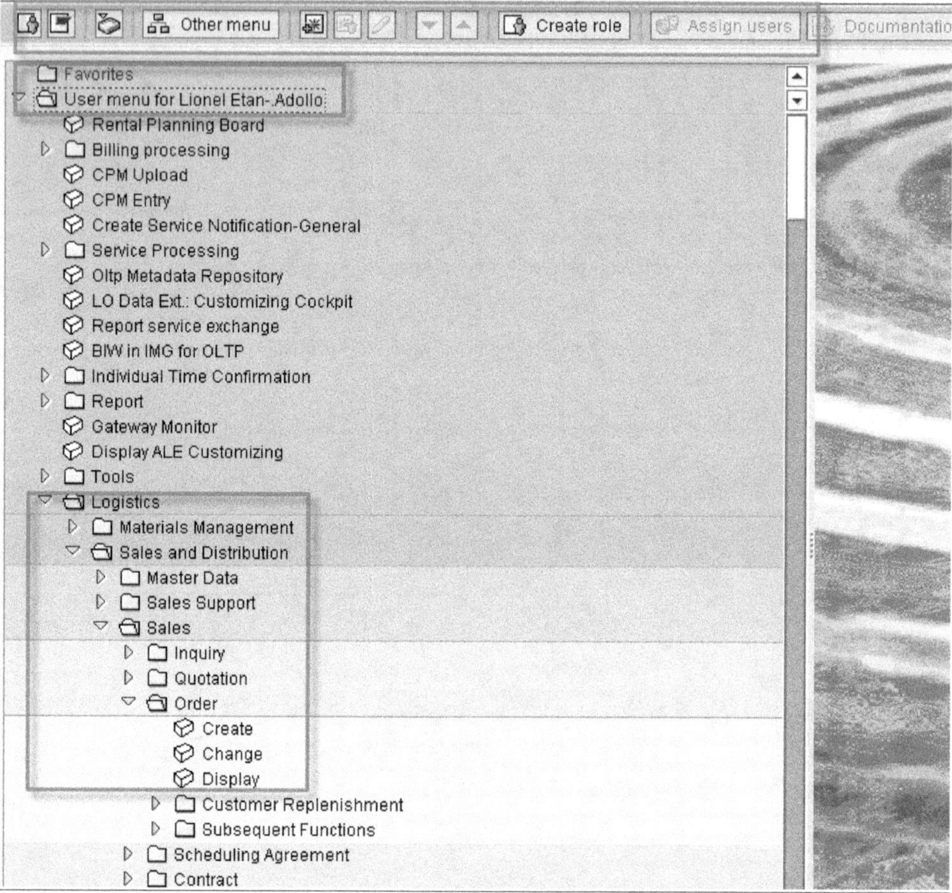

I.V. Using transaction codes

Once you have understood the above simple process steps and logic, it is therefore understandable for you, the beginner, to know that entering transaction code VA01 in the transaction code box and clicking on the green mark symbol on the left of the transaction code box shown in Figure I.XI will appropriately take you to the first screen in the sales order creation process. We will be using the Sales and Distribution module and the applicable documents therein for a lot of our examples in this book.

Figure I.XI **Using transaction codes in** *the SAP Easy Access or any an SAP R/3 screen*

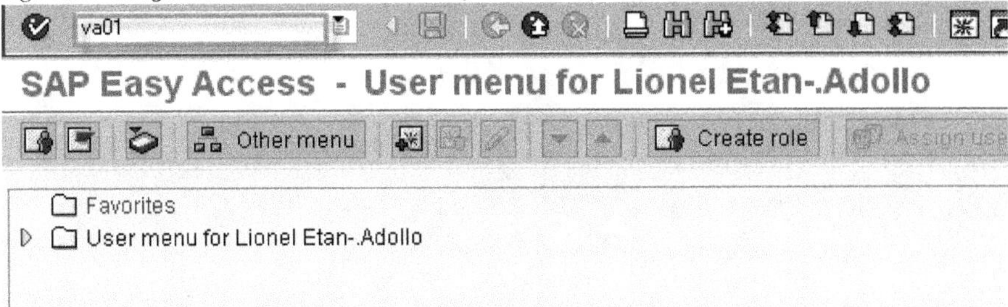

VA01 takes you to

Figure I.XII   Sales Order creation initial screen

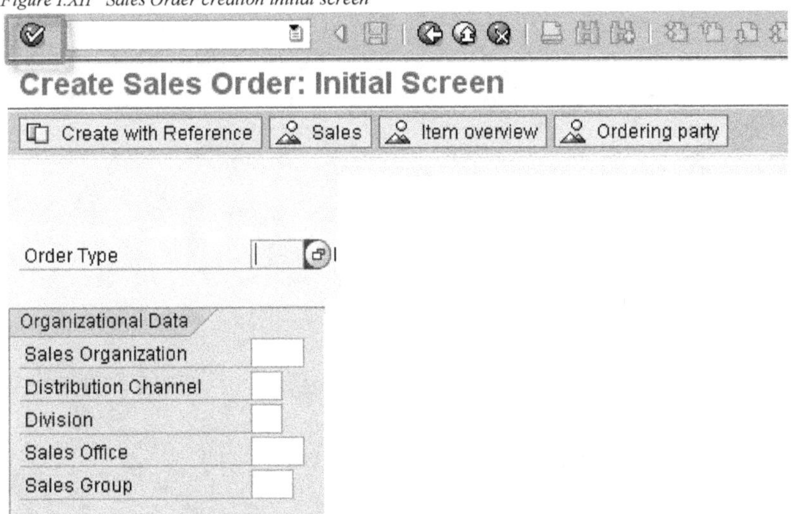

For the process designer (an SAP R/3 functional consultant specialist), setting up the Order types (for example, the Sales Activity document, Inquiry document or the Sales Order document) and the Organisational data configuration (*customizing*) steps correctly is paramount (See *Figure III.III Configuration (Customizing) Steps*). If you don't get it right, you and your process users maybe stuck in processing your document completely. For example, if you were working with the Sales Order creation initial screen, you may not be able to proceed to the next screen (the sales document) if master data is not set up correctly. Setting up the necessary master data right is also core to a good sales document that meets the specific need of a business and sales organisation.

Hopefully, once your customizing is successful and you put in your specific order type, sales organisation, distribution channel and division and click you get into the sales document (Create Standard Order: Overview screen).

Figure I.X III Create Standard Order: Overview

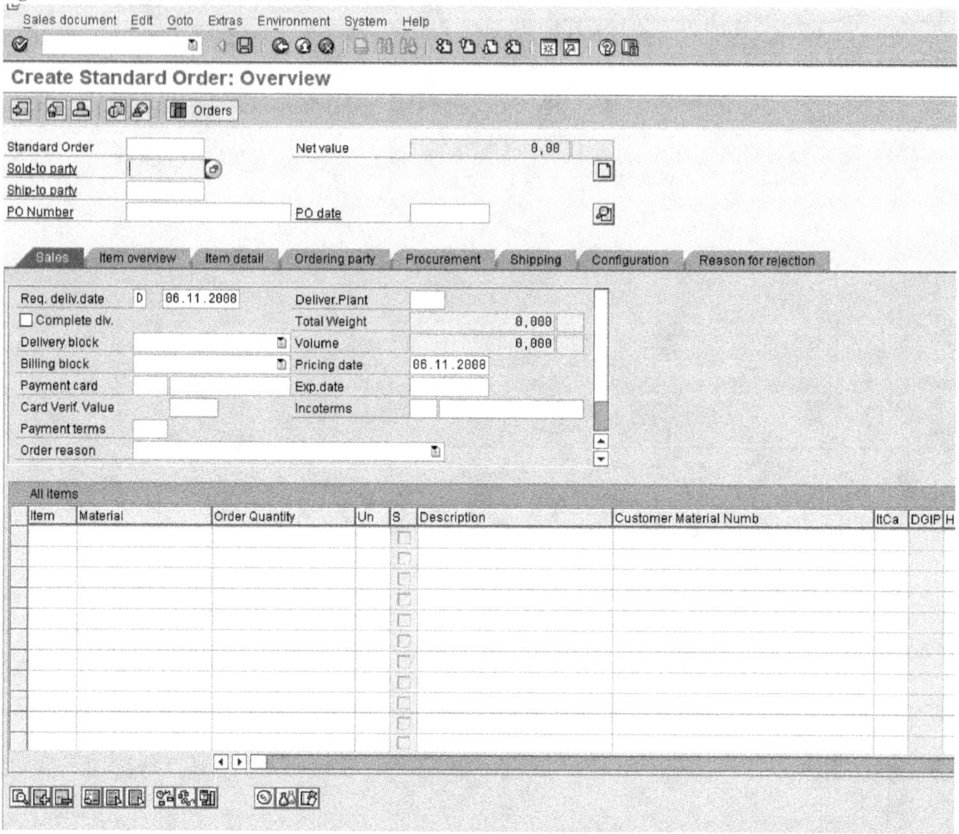

Create Standard Order: Overview

Also, you can input into the transaction code box another transaction code, which will take you to another document to process or display.

In the next chapter, we will now discuss some of the master data set up necessary for the successful functioning of the sales document and processes.

I.VI Lessons from the Conglomerates and Transborder Corporations

In conglomerates and transborder corporations, the System Administrator is able to define the extent of access and authorization you have in the system.

Chapter Two: Master data set up

You are now settled at work and in your Sales Order document. You need to be able to quickly understand how important information such as your customers' sold to party, ship to party, bill to party, materials, payment terms, order reasons, shipping, plants, storage locations and billing are set up. You need to be able to quickly set up these core data in your system or make changes to them whenever required. On this master data, the system processes rely. If you get your data mapping wrong your processes and project will not be successful. See example of customer and material master record (Figure II.I and Figure II.II); this is where you set up the required data information.

Also, you need to understand as a consultant why you are required to store certain data for customers, material and other organisational and financial key structures in your master data set up, or design your documents and processes according to certain guidelines and conventions. This is usually to meet certain legal and fiscal requirements. For example: (i) *Sales Requirements:* Documentation of inquiries, quotations, sales, delivery and scheduling agreements, invoicing, and increase visibility into customer demands and market dynamics; (ii) *Government Requirements:* For example in the sales area, import and exporting companies are expected to document import and export (*excise guidelines*) at all times; (iii) *Tax Authorities Requirements: Ad valorem,* Value Added Tax (VAT) & Pricing guidelines; (iv) *External Reporting Requirements:* Financial accounting and regulatory requirements by government, companies house and tax authorities; (v) *Real Time Visibility into Company's Financial Operations:* Investment banks and Mergers and Acquisition (M&A) specialists are asking for real time visibility into companies' financial operations; (vi) *Internal Reporting Requirements:* Also required for internal management and financial accounting requirements; (vii) *Vendor Requirements:* Materials and stocks documentation. Also strengthen relationships with trade partners to ensure better service and responsiveness to retailer mandates; (viii) *Joint Venture Requirements:* As it affects management of plants, storage locations, margins, transportation, and share of profit between joint venture partners; (ix) *Competition:* To gain competitive edge against competitors by streamlining operations and IT across the organisation; (x) *Setting Up Appropriate Naming Conventions and Documentation Across the Organisation*; (xi) *Health and Safety Requirements:* Government now requires companies (i.e. oil and gas companies) to embed compliance and product safety into core business processes.

SAP R/3 software for enterprise resource planning has a full range of capabilities to meet all of these requirements.

As you will realise, working with an SAP R/3 system is not just about setting up the system, but takes a matured business mindset and thought process, in order to understand and satisfy the needs and requirements of the business and stakeholders, which is paramount.

Always avoid overwriting information and data records already created in the system. Create your own data or make a copy of what is already in the system, and thereafter make your own changes and test. For example, if customer LEA1 is already created in the system, you don't just go ahead making changes to the customer, without instructions to do so. Always document data changes and new data creation when instructed and approved by your organisation.

When setting up your key data structure, I usually prefer creating a new data record as a copy of an old one or another similar data record already in the system and then make changes to it. For example, customers, materials, equipments, vendors, plants etc. You can create a new customer with a unique customer data identifier if there are no business conventions for doing this, but this is unlikely. In Figure II.I we create a new customer data called BBB123. We get to this screen through the following menu path: *Logistic > Sales and Distribution > Master Data > Customer.*

Figure II.1 Create Customer data

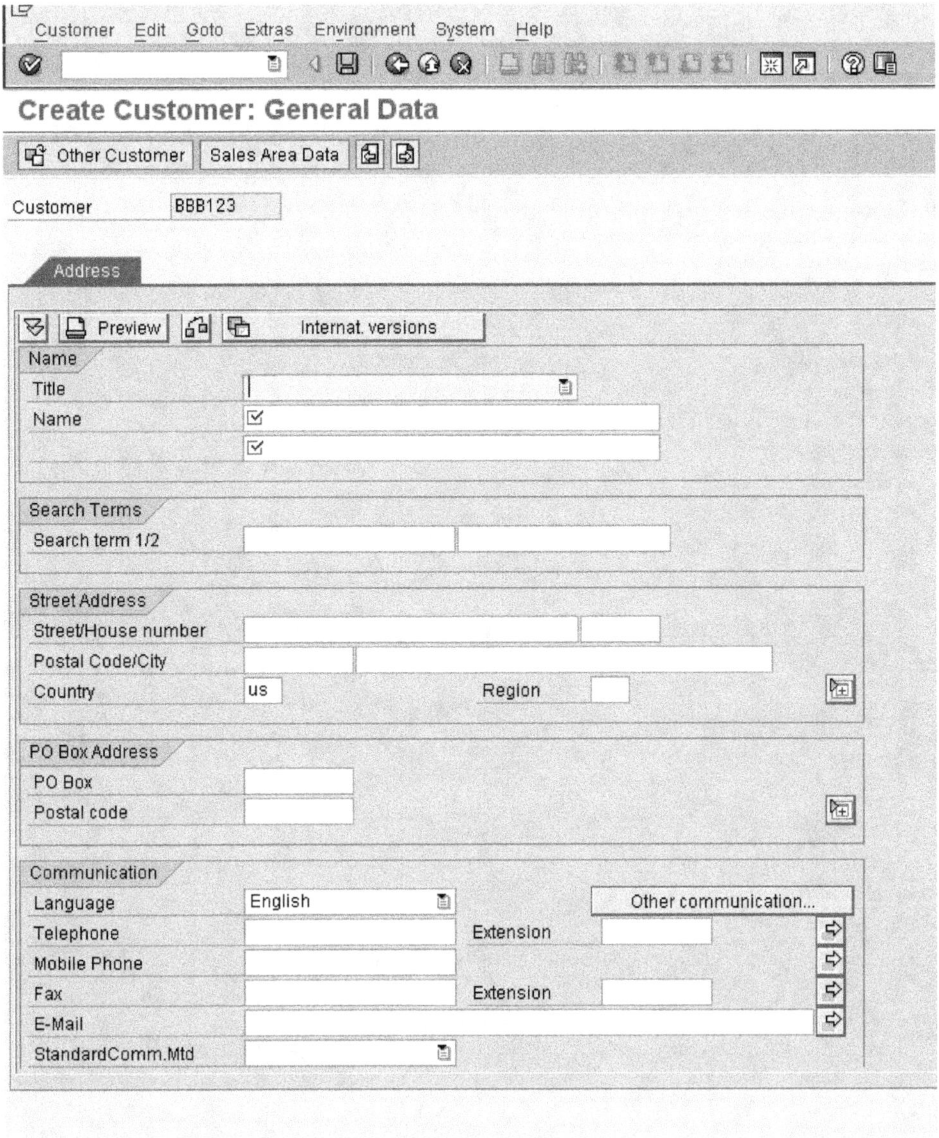

You can create a new material with a unique material data identifier if there are no business conventions for doing this, but this is unlikely. In Figure II.II we create a material data called BB34. We get to this screen through the following menu path: *Logistic >Master Data > Material Master > Material.*

Figure II.II Create Material data

It is only when the customer record (following the menu path or using transaction code VD01) and the material record (following the menu path or using transaction code MM01) are created and saved that you can now use the customer (BBB123) and the material (BB34) in your sales document.

II.III Test your master data within the context of the defined business processes

Make sure you test your customer and the material in your sales document. The Create Standard Order: Overview document should pick up your customer and material created, if created properly. Furthermore, you should be able to save Create Standard Order: Overview document successfully, having completed it with all necessary data and information required.

Figure II.III Create Standard Order: Overview (Customer and Material data highlighted)

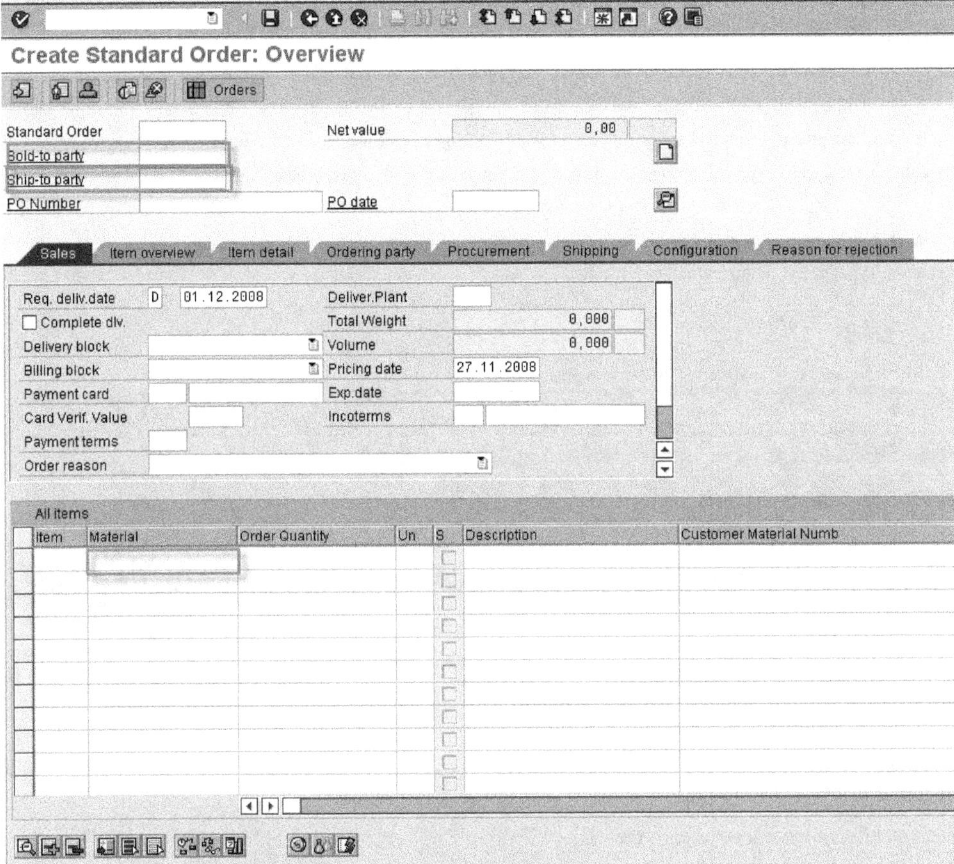

II.IV Your data MUST be correctly set up

If your data is not correctly set up, your processes (including your sales document) cannot run smoothly and there is a high likelihood your project will not succeed.

In the next chapter, we will discuss some of the configuration set up necessary for the successful functioning of the sales document.

II.V Lessons from the Conglomerates and Transborder Corporations

In most conglomerates and transborder corporations, master data will be set up centrally, preferably using SAP master data solution Master Data Management (MDM).

Chapter Three: Working through the Configuration Menu paths step by step

<u>*III.I Familiarise yourself with the menu paths*</u>

It is still your first day or first few days at work, and you have just been instructed by your process team leader or colleague that you will be ultimately responsible for the creation of new sales document order types, defining item categories and schedule lines, and making further changes to them in your SD project, because there are few business requirements and deliverables in this area and you will have to handle this part. You do not need to sweat or be frightened !

The aim of configuration (*customizing*) is to map the standard system to the needs and requirements of the specific organisation. Type in **spro** in the transaction code box.

Figure III.I Accessing Configuration (Customizing) Steps

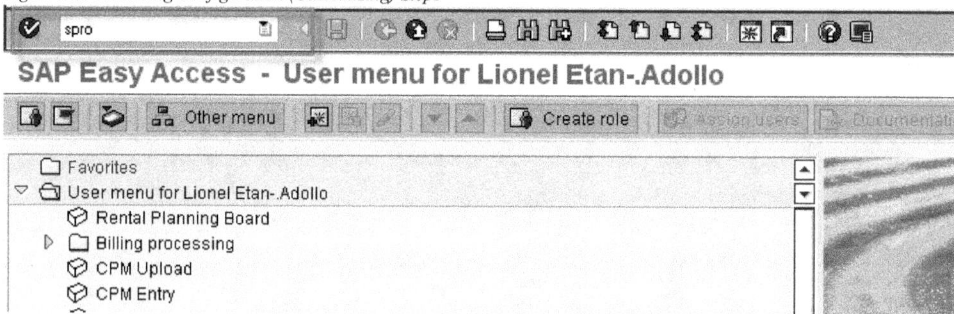

Click on SAP Reference IMG in the next sreen which takes you to the structure of the IMG Implementation Guide

Figure III.II Configuration (Customizing) Steps

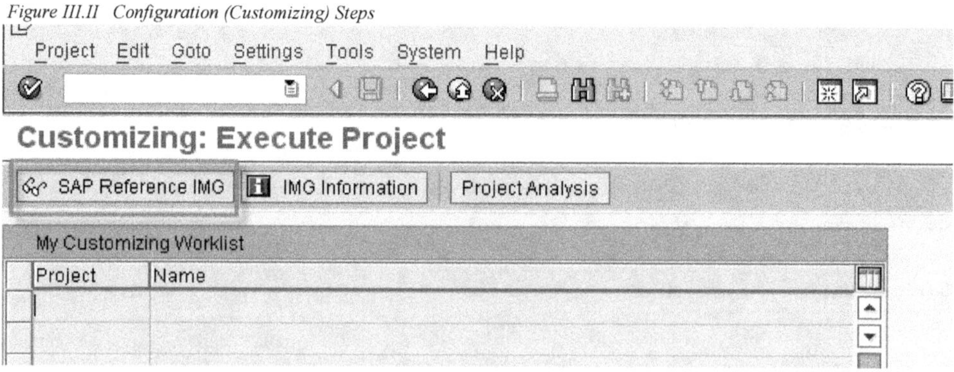

In Figures III.III to III.VII, you can see step by step layout of the configuration (customizing) procedure of some of the SAP R/3 modules we have shown below.

Figure III.III   Step by Step layout of the Configuration (Customizing) procedure for the Financial Accounting module

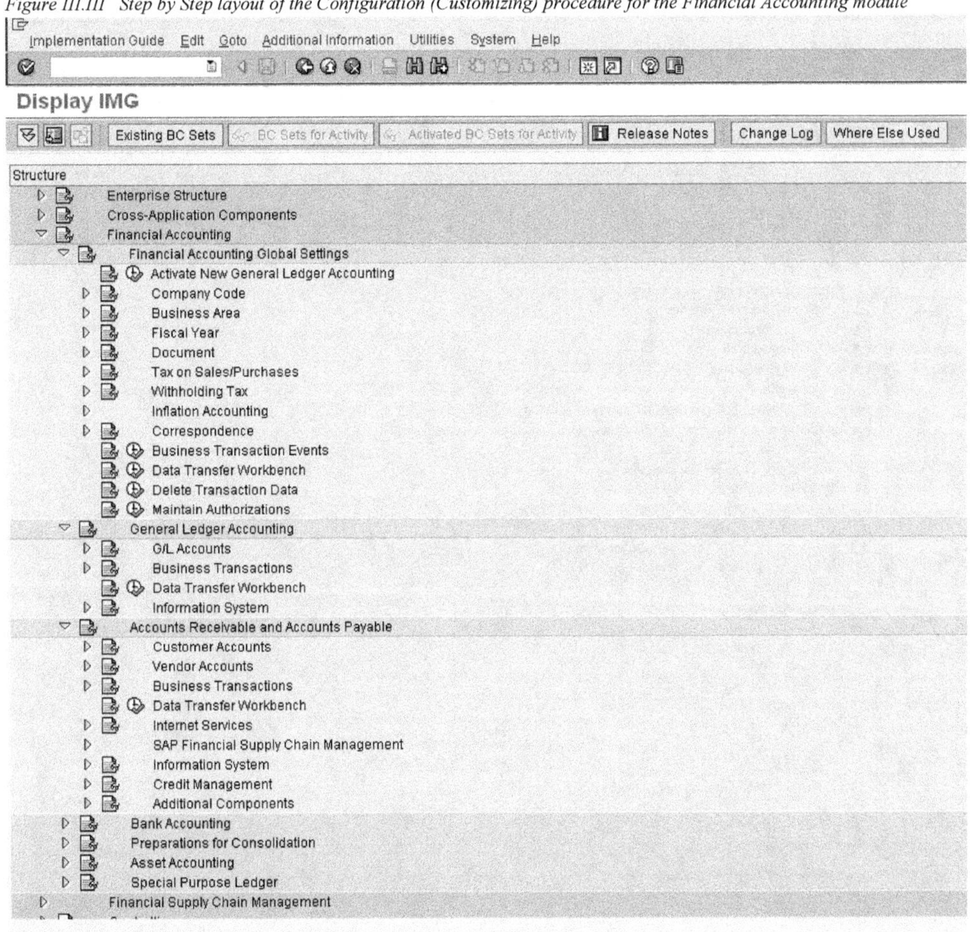

Figure III.IV   Step by Step layout of the Configuration (Customizing) procedure for the Sales and Distribution module

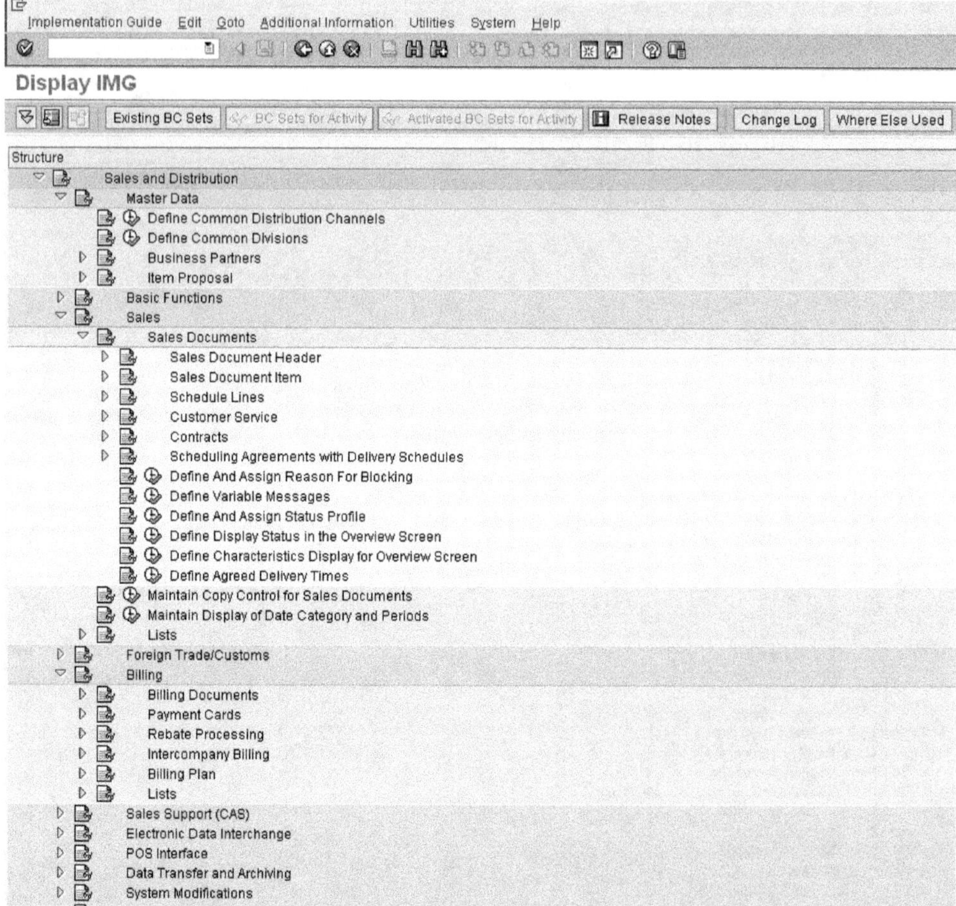

Figure III.V   Step by Step layout of the Configuration (Customizing) procedure for Customer Service and Plant Maintenance module

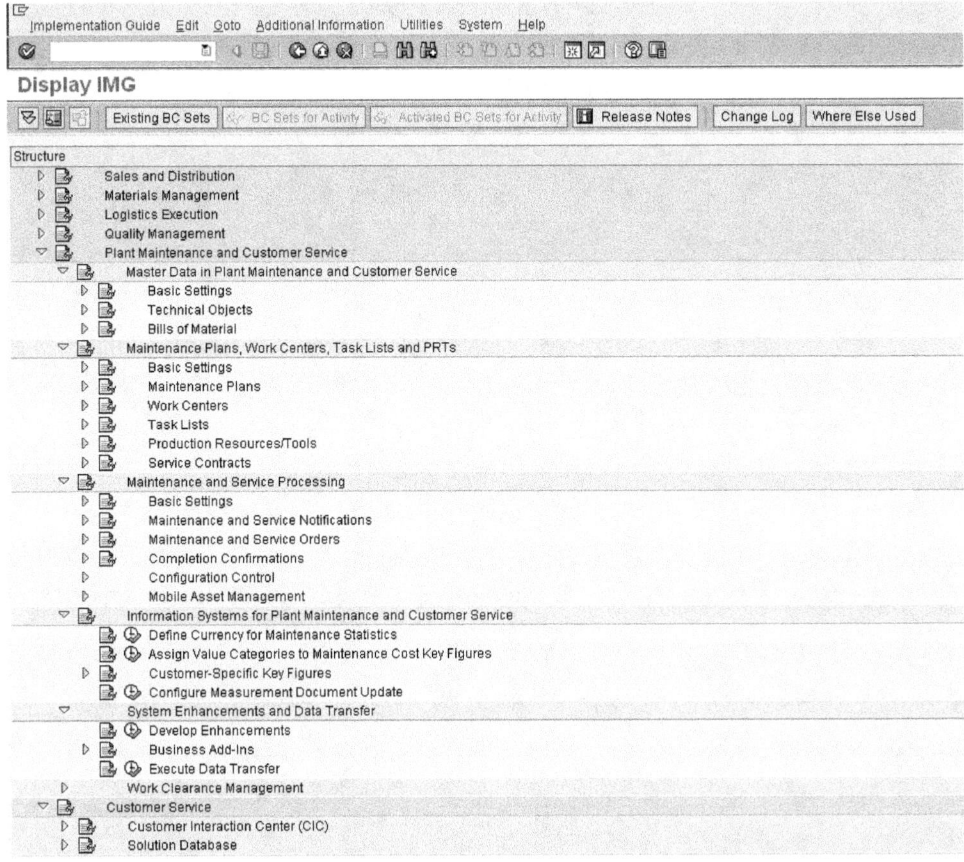

Customizing (IMG) for Industry Solution Oil and Gas (Downstream, PRA and Remote Logistic Management):

Figure III.VI   Step by Step layout of the Configuration (Customizing) procedure for the Industry Solution Oil and Gas (IS-OIL) module (1)

Display IMG

| | Existing BC Sets | BC Sets for Activity | Activated BC Sets for Activity | Release Notes | Change Log | Where Else Used |

Structure

- ▽ Joint Venture Accounting
  - Activate JVA in a Client
  - ▷ Environment
  - ▷ Master Data
  - ▷ Processing
  - ▷ Billing
  - ▷ Non-operated
  - ▷ Tools
  - ▷ Project Risk Management for Contractors
- ▽ Industry Solution Oil & Gas (Downstream)
  - ▷ Integration with Customer Relationship Management
  - ▷ Cross-Application Components
  - ▷ HPM (Hydrocarbon Product Management)
  - ▷ TDP (Tariffs, Duties and Permits)
  - ▷ EXG (Exchanges)
  - ▷ TD (Transportation and Distribution)
  - ▷ MAP (Marketing, Accounting and Pricing)
  - ▷ MCOE (Marketing, Contracts and Order Entry)
  - ▷ MRN (Marketing Retail Network)
  - ▷ SSR (Service Station Retailing)
  - ▷ BDRP (Bulk Distribution Requirements Planning)
  - ▷ TSW (Trader's and Scheduler's Workbench)
  - ▷ OGSD (Secondary Distribution)
- ▽ Industry Solution Oil & Gas (PRA)
  - ▷ Global Settings
  - ▷ Ownership
  - ▷ Contracts and Pricing
  - ▷ Production
  - ▷ Sales and Balancing
  - ▷ Revenue Accounting
  - ▷ Production, Tax and Royalty Reporting
  - ▷ Partitioned Data Management (PDM)

Figure III.VII   Step by Step layout of the Configuration (Customizing) procedure for the Industry Solution Oil and Gas (IS-OIL) module (2)

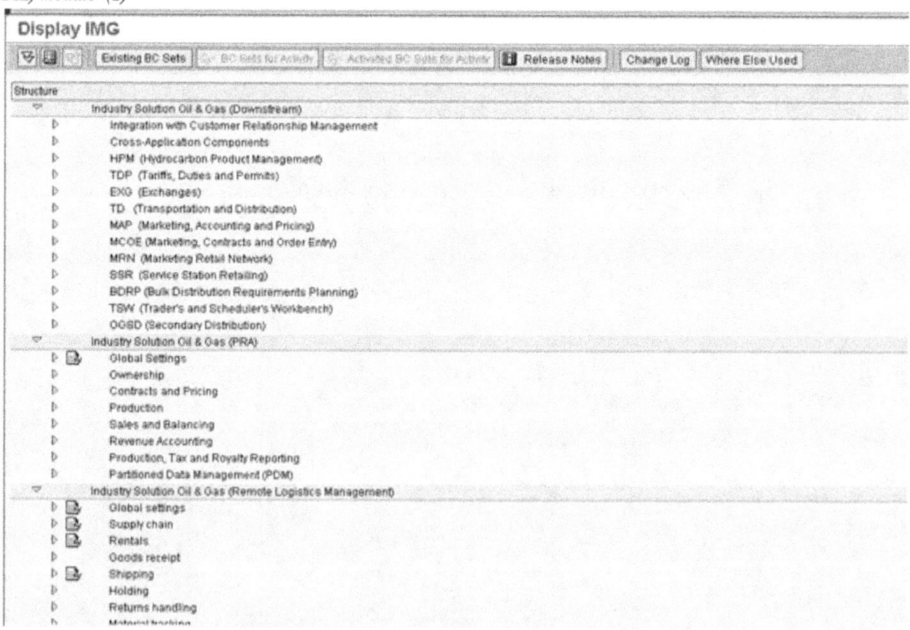

Display IMG

| | Existing BC Sets | BC Sets for Activity | Activated BC Sets for Activity | Release Notes | Change Log | Where Else Used |

Structure

- ▽ Industry Solution Oil & Gas (Downstream)
  - ▷ Integration with Customer Relationship Management
  - ▷ Cross-Application Components
  - ▷ HPM (Hydrocarbon Product Management)
  - ▷ TDP (Tariffs, Duties and Permits)
  - ▷ EXG (Exchanges)
  - ▷ TD (Transportation and Distribution)
  - ▷ MAP (Marketing, Accounting and Pricing)
  - ▷ MCOE (Marketing, Contracts and Order Entry)
  - ▷ MRN (Marketing Retail Network)
  - ▷ SSR (Service Station Retailing)
  - ▷ BDRP (Bulk Distribution Requirements Planning)
  - ▷ TSW (Trader's and Scheduler's Workbench)
  - ▷ OGSD (Secondary Distribution)
- ▽ Industry Solution Oil & Gas (PRA)
  - ▷ Global Settings
  - ▷ Ownership
  - ▷ Contracts and Pricing
  - ▷ Production
  - ▷ Sales and Balancing
  - ▷ Revenue Accounting
  - ▷ Production, Tax and Royalty Reporting
  - ▷ Partitioned Data Management (PDM)
- ▽ Industry Solution Oil & Gas (Remote Logistics Management)
  - ▷ Global settings
  - ▷ Supply chain
  - ▷ Rentals
  - ▷ Goods receipt
  - ▷ Shipping
  - ▷ Holding
  - ▷ Returns handling
  - ▷ Material tracking

Joint Venture Accounting:

Activate JVA in a Client; Environment; Master data; Processing; Billing; Non-operated; Tools; Project Risk management for Contractors.

Industry Solution Oil and Gas (Downstream):

Integration with Customer Relationship Management; Cross Application Components; HPM (Hydrocarbon Product Management); TDP (Tariffs, Duties and Permits); EXG (Exchanges); TD (Transportation and Distribution); MAP (Marketing, Accounting and Pricing); MCOE (Marketing, Contracts and Order Entry); MRN (Marketing Retail Network); SSR (Service Station Retailing); BDRP (Bulk Distribution Requirements Planning); TSW (Trader's and Scheduler's Workbench); OGSD (Secondary Distribution)

Industry Solution Oil and Gas (PRA):

Global Settings; Ownership; Contracts and Pricing; Production; Sales and Balancing; Revenue Accounting; Production, Tax and Royalty Reporting; Partitioned Data Management (PDM)

Industry Solution Oil and Gas (Remote Logistics Management):

Global Settings; Supply Chain; Rentals; Goods Receipt; Shipping; Holding; Returns Handling; Material Tracking

For a detailed understanding of how to customize an SAP R/3 system, register for an appropriate training course with www.sap.com

III.II The principle is that configuration set up is done step by step for all core modules

Always do your configuration (customizing) in the development client or play system (for example, sandbox) and never in the production client. Familiarise yourself again with *Figure I.II Entering Specific SAP Client and User Identification* and the various client(s) set up. Do not be afraid to ask questions from your System Administrator and colleagues when you are not clear about which client and system to use for your configuration and also test your configuration. You also need to clarify the *transport* procedure (that is how data is moved from one client to another) in the organisation; the procedure is different in a lot of organisations. See section ***III.VII Understand how to transport your configuration and development design from the development client to other clients.***

For all core SAP R/3 modules, understand that configuration (*customizing*) is done from the top down.

In customizing your sales document, on the sales document header level: (a) you define your sales document types; (b) convert language for each sales document type if the organisation is a cross county or global organisation; (c) define number ranges for sales documents; (d) define purchase order types; (e) define order reasons; (f) define usage indicators, (g) assign sales area to sales document types.

Today, multinational corporations and conglomerates that invest hugely in SAP R/3, SAP Solution Manager will handle documentation and design/process management (for example, solution design both functional and technical; approval processes and tasks; and also the transport procedure for both system and process changes) in the organisation. Some SAP R/3 consultants are specialists in this area.

Figure III.VIII Sales document header level, item level and schedule lines configuration

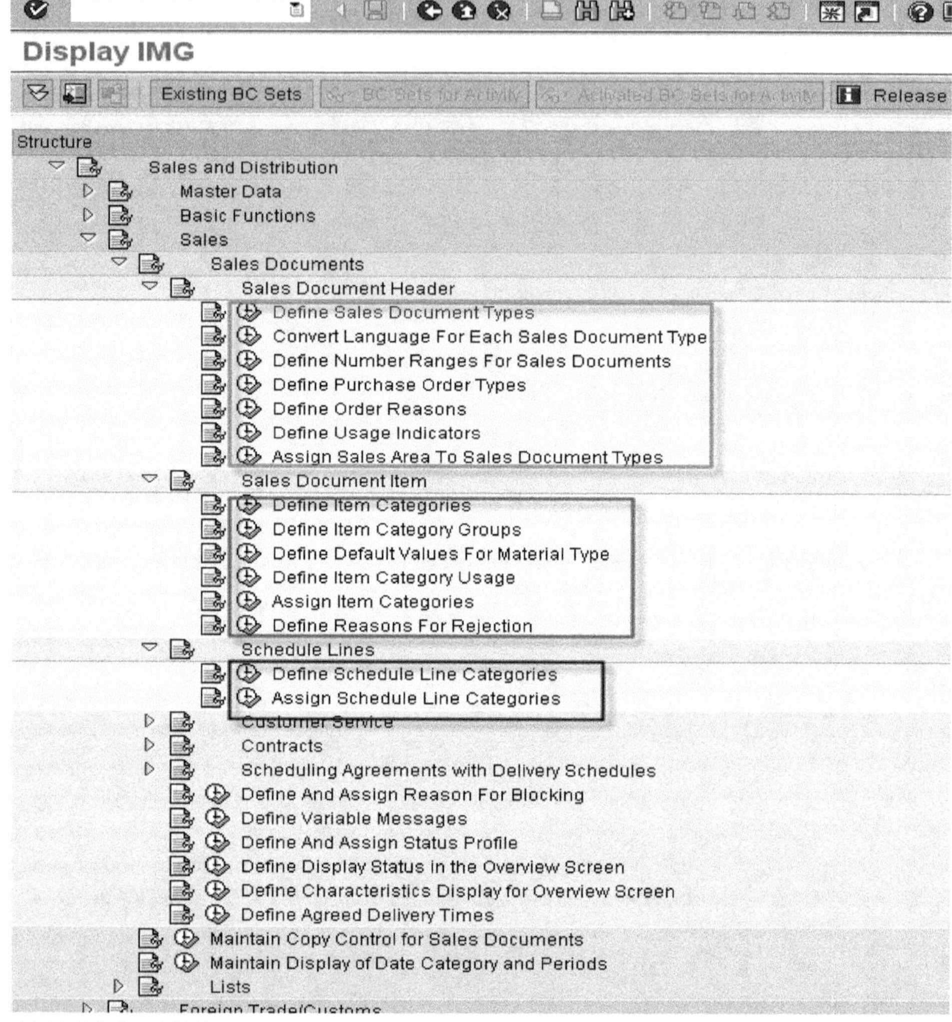

Once you have completed the sales document header level, you then start your step-by-step configuration for both the sales document item and schedule lines.

On the sales document item level: (a) you define the item categories; (b) define item category groups; (c) define default values for material types; (d) define item category usages; (e) assign item categories; (f) define reasons for rejection.

On the sales document schedule lines: (a) define schedule line categories; (b) assign schedule line categories.

III.III Always copy an SAP R/3 configuration top down to create your own configuration

Always copy SAP R/3 standard configuration settings or your organisation's configuration settings, top down, to create your own customizing. Do not delete standard configuration and settings in the system. Deletion may affect other areas of the system, for example tables and fields relating to other areas in the system. Also set up and test your configuration in the appropriate client.

III.IV Some settings are cross client

Changes in one area of the system may have implications in other areas of the system. Some customizing changes you make centrally in accounting may have implications in the sales and distribution area. Hence, be aware that some settings are cross client and you must learn to communicate and share knowledge in an SAP R/3 environment.

III.V Make your configuration clear and simple to understand, particularly your naming conventions and descriptions

Always make your configuration clear and simple to understand, particularly your naming conventions and descriptions. This is always good for identification and searches in an SAP R/3 system. Always clarify with your organisation the naming convention for customers, materials, plants, storage locations, profit centres etc.

It is always absurd to spend a lot of money and time setting up the system without much thought on what is best for the organisation in terms of naming conventions.

III.VI Always test your configurations and make sure it does not affect other areas, and if it does, share impact with fellow consultants responsible for areas affected

Always test your configurations so that they work. There is no point setting up configurations that do not work. Also, always discuss impact with fellow consultants working with other modules as it concerns them too.

III.VII Understand how to transport your configuration and development design from the development client to other clients

Understand how to transport your configuration from the development client to other clients. For example, learn how to transport to other development sub-system; quality client and sub-system; and finally to the production system.

Step 1: In general terms, once your configuration is saved, you create your *transport request*. You give your request a description according to the business convention and then you save your request. Remember to record your request number.
Step 2: In this case we will also permit that you use transaction code SE10, there you can see your saved request number. Click on *modifiable* and not *released* so that you can still put things in it if required.
Step 3: In this case we will also permit that you use transaction code SCC1 (in your development client). Put in your request number and also tick including *request subtasks* and *test run*. Press *start immediately*. Click *Yes* to copy client-specific data from your development client to another client (for example, another development client, quality assurance client or production client). The system will give you the information that program ran successfully (go back and you see: *copy by transport request*).

Step 4: Then go back to transaction code SPRO in your development client and see that configuration is copied correctly.

Step 5: Test your new configuration in your development client. Once satisfied, go to step 6.

Step 6: Once satisfied with the configuration, finally transport number removing the tick against test run.

To search for transports, in this case go to transaction code STMS and click on transport overview and your transport should be displayed. Alternatively, you can go to transaction SE01 (Transport Organizer for user, in this case EXTLIET). Transaction SE01 gives more details on the transport in the destination client (other development sub-system; quality client and sub-system; and finally to the production system).

In the next chapter, we will discuss understanding the core business processes of your organisation and the SAP R/3 module(s) you are working in; in our case study some areas of the Sales and Distribution module and some areas of other related modules (Materials Management, Customer Service/ Service Management, Industry Solution – Oil and Gas).

III.VIII Lessons from the Conglomerates and Transborder Corporations

Today, multinational corporations and conglomerates that invest hugely in an SAP R/3 system, will handle documentation and design/process management (for example, solution design both functional and technical; approval processes and tasks; and also the transport procedure for both system and process changes) using SAP Solution Manager in their organisation.

Chapter Four: Understand the business processes and conduct several tests

IV.1 Run through many system tests to understand the business processes

You have now set up your master data (or key data structure) and configuration settings in line with the business requirements. Your other teammates, also SD Consultants, have set up the delivery and billing documents master data and necessary configuration, and the question now arises: will the sales business processes pass the end-to-end testing required?

With the Sales and Distribution module, the core business processes are: *Sales Activity, Inquiry, Quotation, Sales Order, Delivery, and Billing* documents. Bear in mind that not all businesses use all these core processes. In fact in some countries and businesses, you may have inquiry, quotation, billing, sales order and then the delivery process. In some cases, this core SD business process may be intertwined with other SAP R/3 documents (for example, Notification and Service Order documents in the Customer Service module) and records (for example, Vendor and Material Master Records in the Material Management module) to meet certain business requirements.

Figure IV.1   Sales Activity Document (Sales and Distribution module)

Sales Activity document (transaction: VC01n):

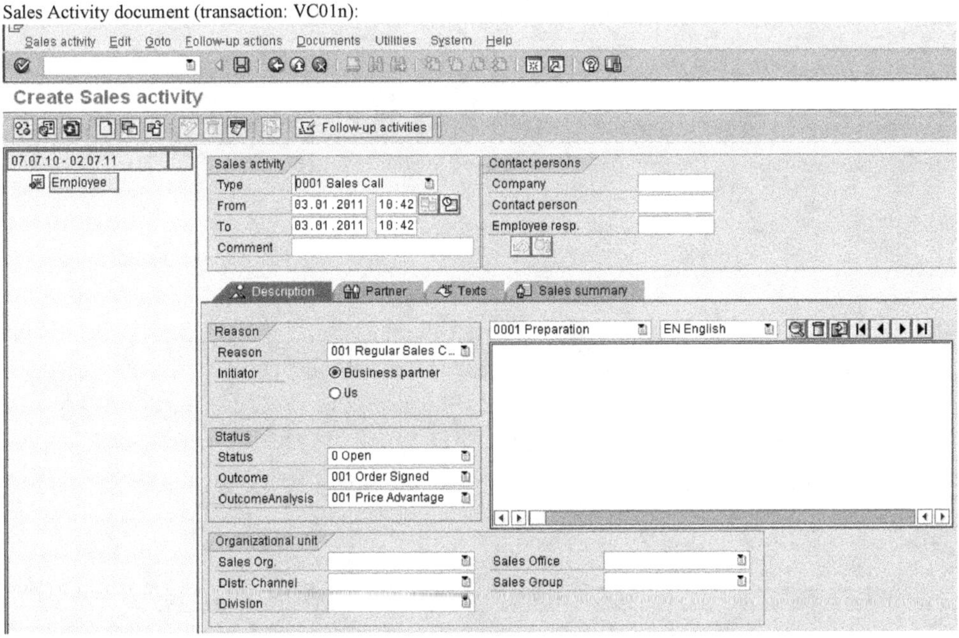

Figure IV.II Inquiry Document (Sales and Distribution module)

Inquiry document (VA11):

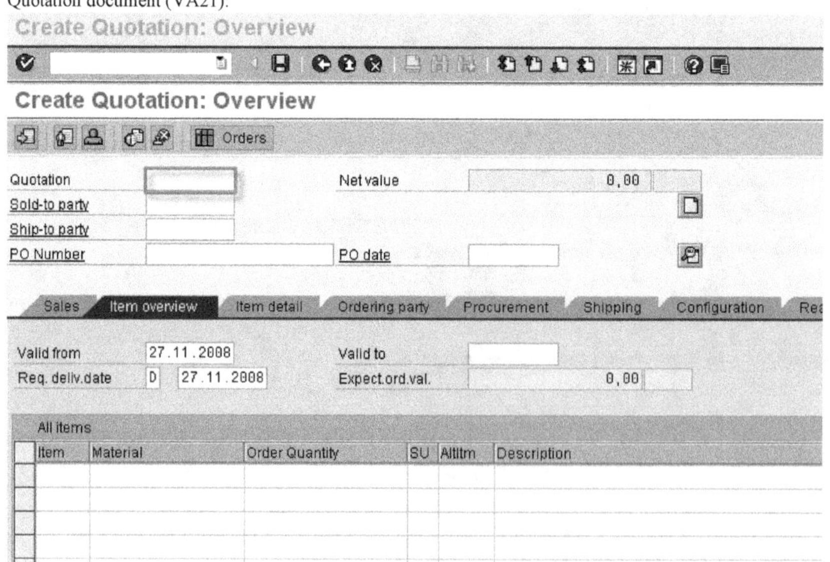

Figure IV.III Quotation Document (Sales and Distribution module)

Quotation document (VA21):

Figure IV.IV   Sales Order Document (Sales and Distribution module)

Sales Order document (VA01):

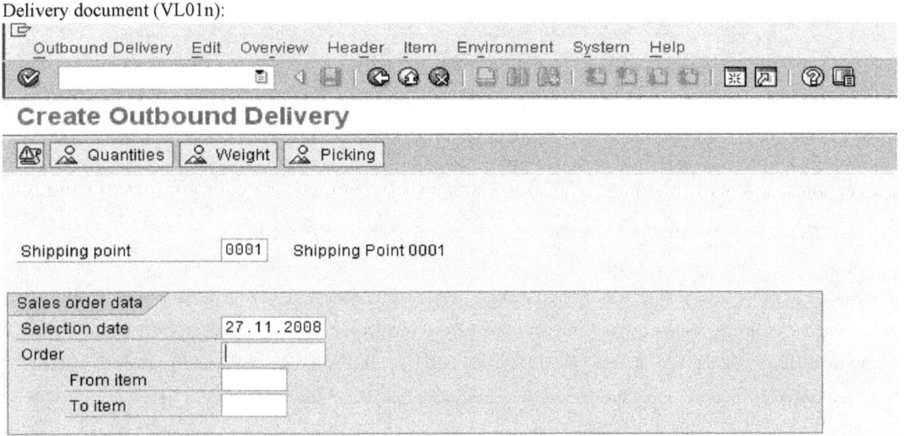

Figure IV.V Delivery Document (Sales and Distribution module)

Delivery document (VL01n):

Figure IV.VI   Billing Document (Sales and Distribution module)

Billing document (VF01):

Create Billing Document

Billing due list | Billing document overview | Selection list

Default data

Billing Type	Serv.rendered
Billing Date	Pricing date

Docs to be processed

Document	Item	SD document categ.	Processing status	Bill

IV.II Reading SAP notes without hands-on business process testing may cause you not to succeed

Hands-on experience and continuous testing of business processes, screens and documents are the hallmark of a good SAP R/3 consultant. Whatever you do, always conduct several tests before you recommend a solution or say a task given to yourself is completed. Hence reading SAP notes without hands-on business process testing may cause you not to succeed. The technology profession is so much about hands-on experience, competence and 'have you done it before!' rather than have you read it (and it is still in your head). The success of the consultant is about what you can do hands-on in the SAP system rather than what you know about the system stored in your head.

Therefore the sandbox and development clients (for development design and configuration) and the test system (or test client) must be your friend.

IV.III Familiarise yourself with different SAP R/3 document types and records that interfaces with SD and logistic processes

You will sometimes have a mix of records and document types (outside of the SD processes) interfaced with your core SD processes.

    (i)   Familiarise yourself with the creation and management of the material master record (transaction MM01).

Figure IV. VII Material Master Record (Materials Management module)

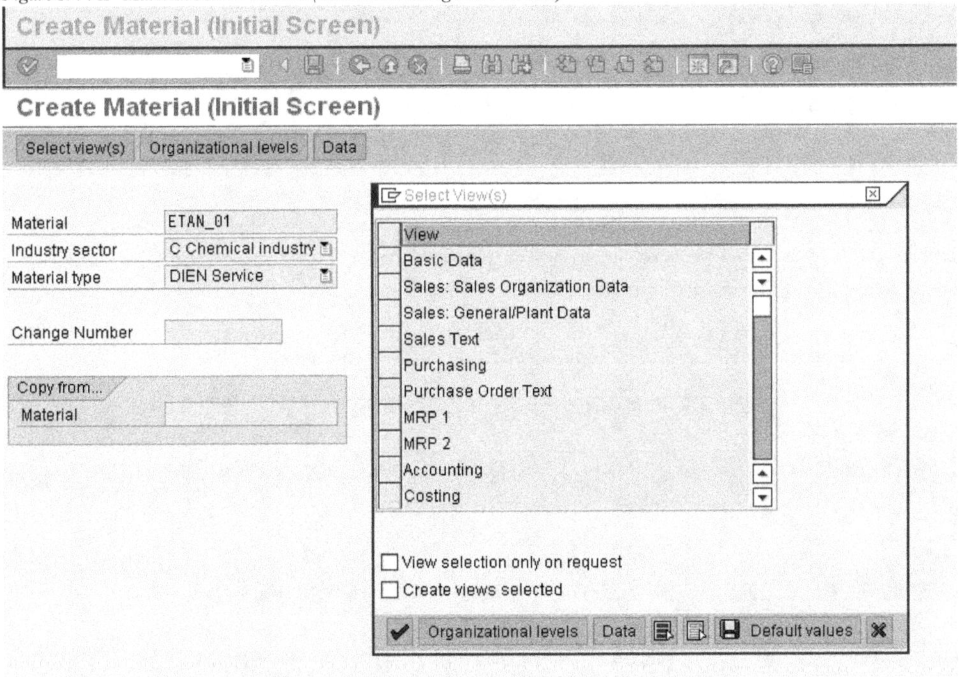

This is where you set up your materials. These materials are used in the SD and Logistic processes.

    (ii)   Familiarise yourself with the creation of Purchase Orders (transaction ME21n). You may need to produce a Purchase Order number before you are able to create a Sales Order document.

Figure IV. VIII   Purchase Order document (Materials Management)

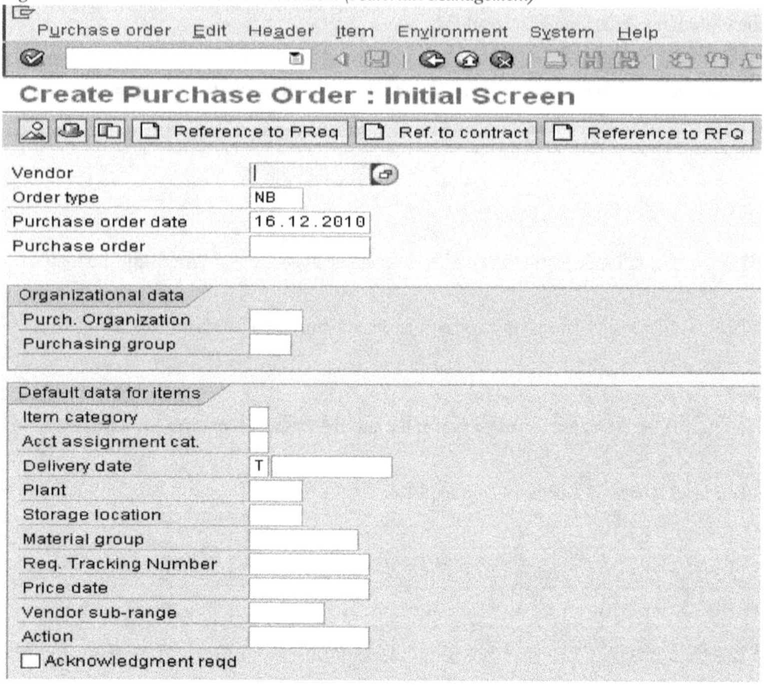

The purchase order number saved may be required as input in your sales document. For example, *Figure IV. VIII* and *Figure IV.IX   Purchase Order number and date input required in Sales document.*

Figure IV. IX   Purchase Order number and date input required in Sales document creation

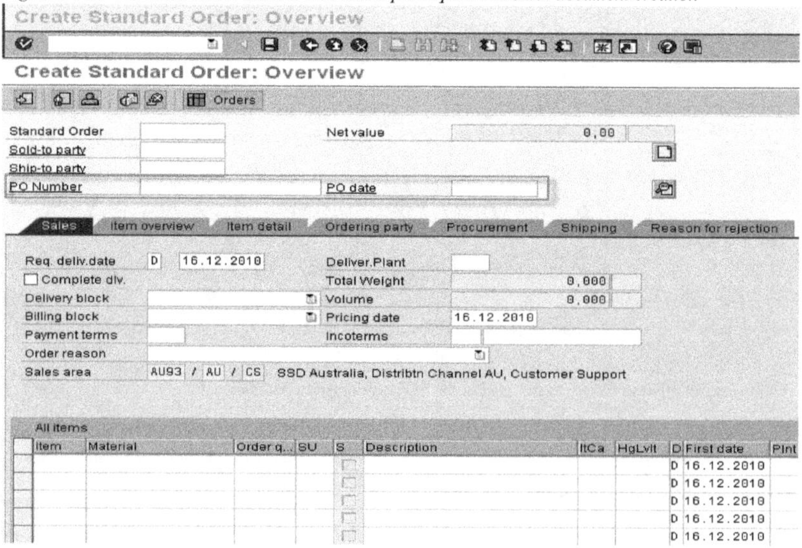

The purchase order number may also be required for Sales Order document change.

Figure IV.X   Purchase Order number and date input required in Sales Order document changes

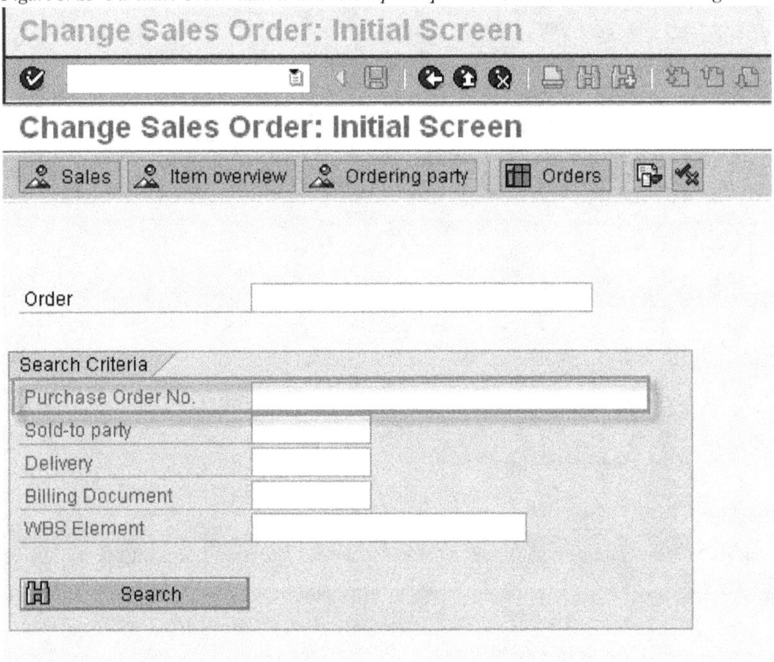

Change Sales Order: Initial Screen

Change Sales Order: Initial Screen

Sales | Item overview | Ordering party | Orders

Order

Search Criteria

Purchase Order No.	
Sold-to party	
Delivery	
Billing Document	
WBS Element	

Search

(iii)   Learn to create Vendor master record (transaction XK01). Your supplier information is required in your Purchase Order document.

Figure IV. XI   Creation of Vendor Records (Materials Management module)

Create Vendor: Initial Screen

Vendor

Company Code

Purch. organization

Account group

Reference

Vendor

Company code

Purch. organization

(iv)   Familiarise yourself with the creation and management of Vendor Info Records (transaction ME11). It is also important that you are able to store information about materials supplied by your vendors for your records.

Figure IV. XIII   Creation of Info Records (Materials Management)

Create Info Record: Initial Screen

Vendor

Material

Purchasing Org.

Plant

Info record

Info category

◉ Standard

○ Subcontracting

○ Pipeline

○ Consignment

(v)   Familiarise yourself with the creation and management of Notification documents (transaction IW51) and Service Order documents (transaction IW31). These two documents are important in a business model design where there are interfaces between Sales and Distribution module and the Customer Service and Plant Maintenance module. Working on Notifications and Service Orders are at the core of Service Management (SM), Plant Maintenance (PM) and Customer Service (CS).

It is not unlikely that you have a business process that starts with sales process (*Sales Activity > Inquiry > Quotation > Sales Order > Delivery > Billing*), and then the conglomerate business also has the opportunity to service the equipment or product sold. This is not uncommon with conglomerates involved with manufacturing of chemicals, health care, electronics, oil and gas, pharmaceuticals and high-tech industries. The business processes could be: *Notification > Service Order > Billing or Sales Order > Service Order > Billing*. When you now have to add purchase of spare parts (materials management module) and also service contract (a Sales Order document type) to this sales and service process, it gets more complicated.

Figure IV. XIV   Creation of Notification documents (Customer Service / Service Management / Plant Maintenance module)

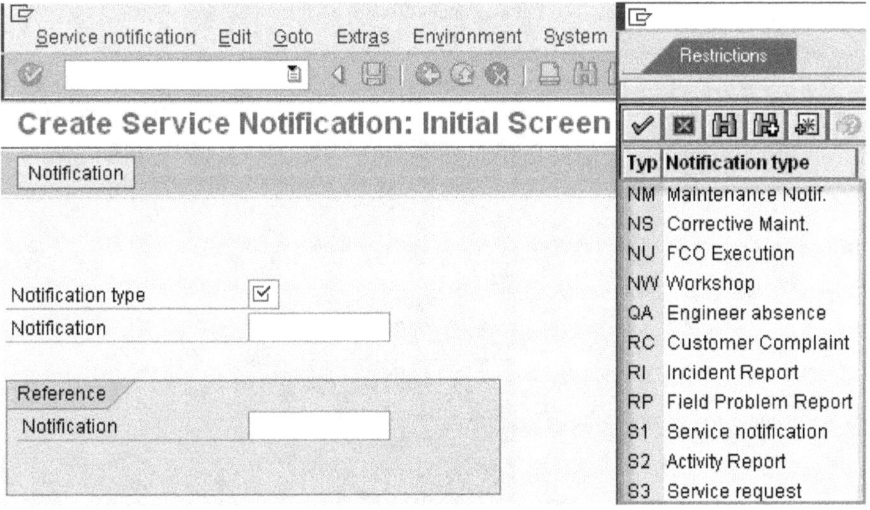

Figure IV. XV   Creation of Service Order document (Customer Service module)

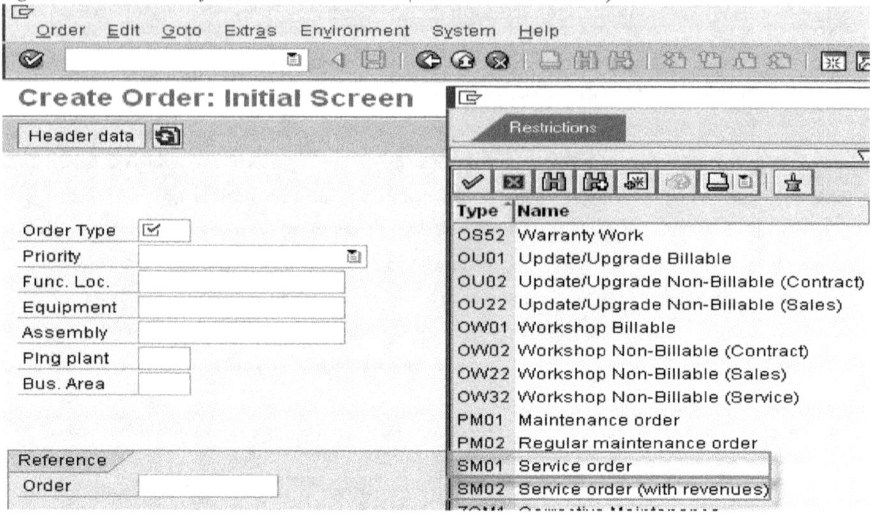

(vi)　　Familiarise yourself with the creation and management of Contract types (transaction VA41). A contract is a Sales Document type, also used by other modules such as Customer Service as service contracts and in Industry Solution - Oil and Gas (IS-OIL) as SAP Exploration and Management Contract Management.

Figure IV. XVI   Creation of Contract document (Sales Order type, also used by other module)

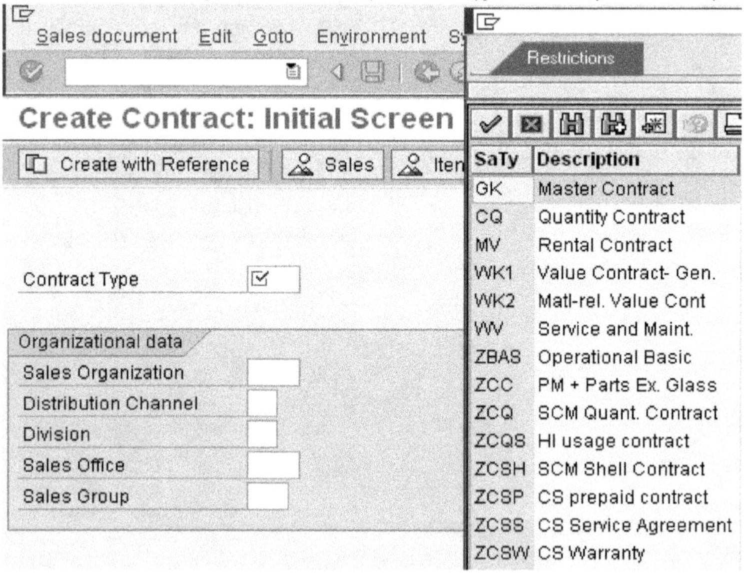

(vii)   Familiarise yourself with the set up and management of Equipments master records (transaction IE01) and Functional Locations (IL01), associated with the Customer Service module.

Figure IV. XVII   Creation of Equipments (Customer Service / Service Management / Plant Maintenance)

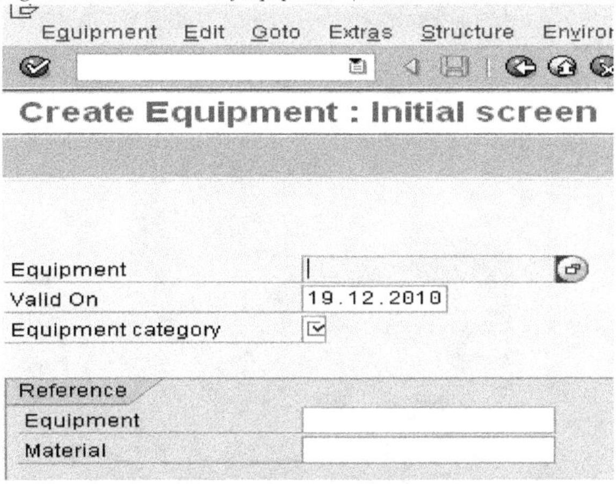

Figure IV. XVIII   Creation of Functional Location (Customer Service / Service Management / Plant Maintenance)

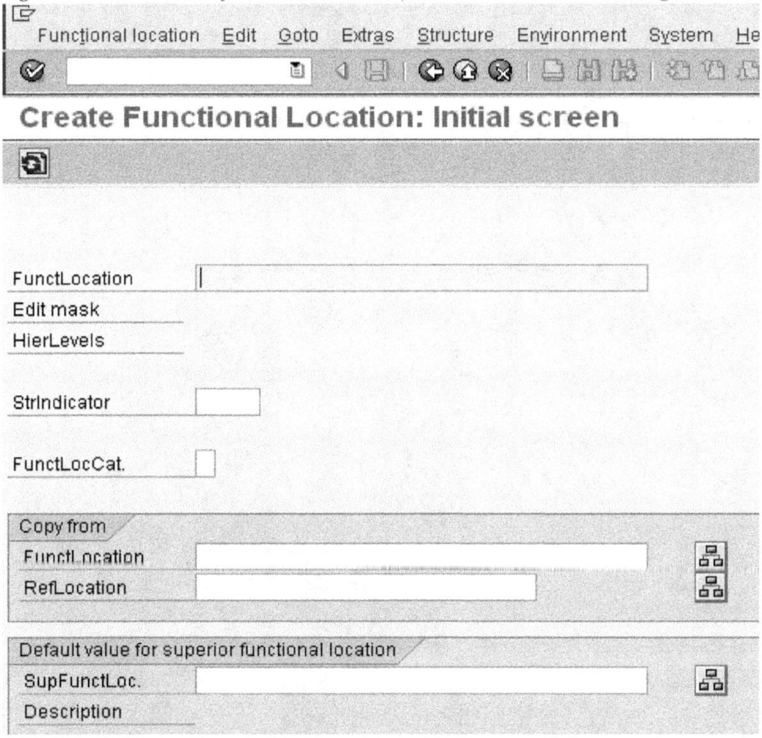

(viii)   On the Industry Solution Oil and Gas frontend we have the *Add-On: Administration and Tools* to the standard SAP R/3 ERP (Enterprise Resource Software):

Figure IV. XIX The IS-OIL Add-on Administration and Tools to the standard SAP R/3 ERP (Enterprise Resource Software) (1)

On the IS-OIL frontend we have the *Add-on Administration and Tools* to the standard SAP R/3 ERP (Enterprise Resource Software):

Figure IV. XX The IS-OIL Add-on Administration and Tools to the standard SAP R/3 ERP (Enterprise Resource Software) (2)

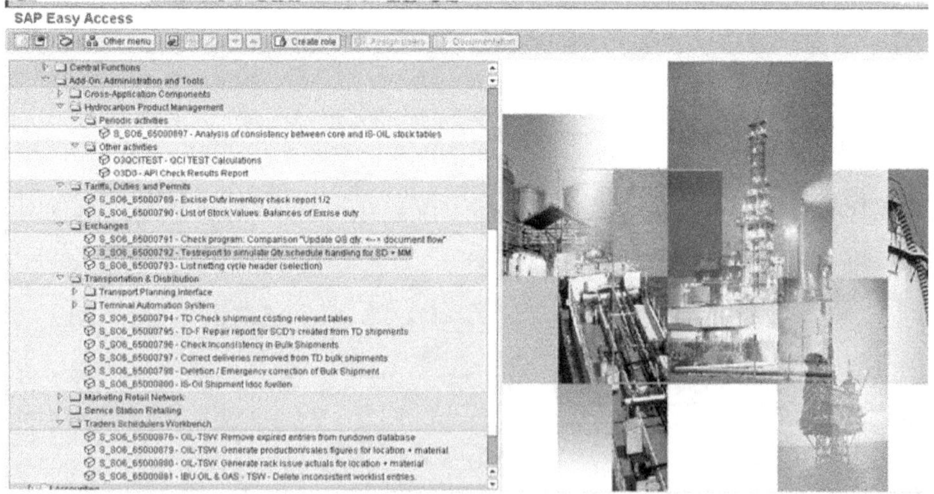

Figure IV. XXI Analysis of consistency between core and IS-OIL stock tables (Periodic Activities) under Hydrocarbon Product Management

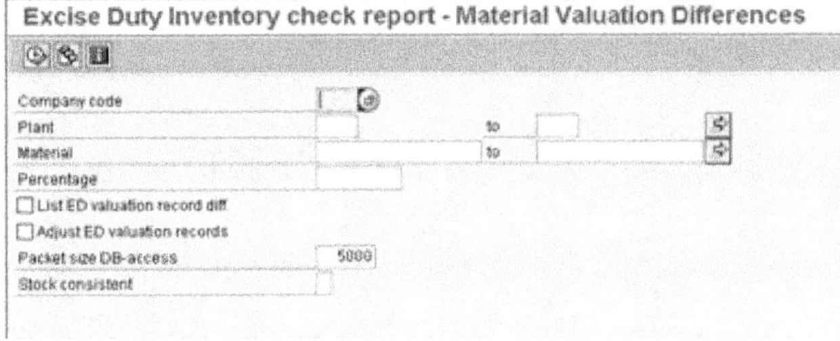

Figure IV. XXII   Excise Duty Inventory check report – Material Valuation (under IS-OIL Tariffs, Duties and Permits)

Figure IV. XXIII   Check TPI document creation (under IS-OIL Transport Planning Interface)

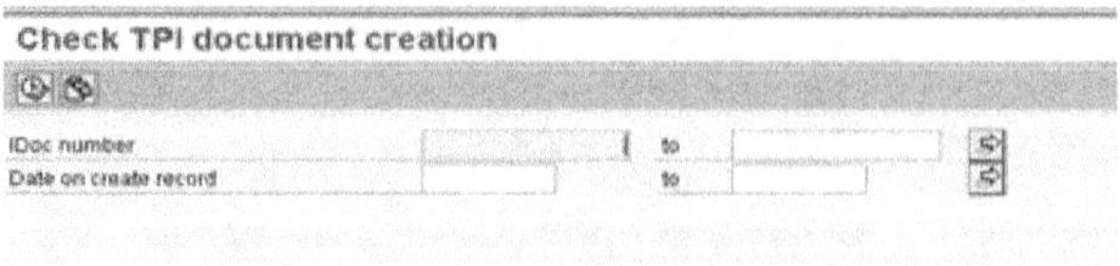

Figure IV. XXIV   Check Inconsistency in bulk Shipments (under IS-OIL Terminal Automation System)

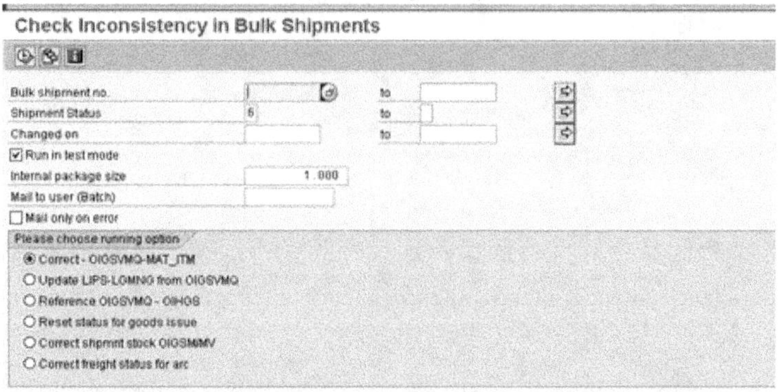

Figure IV. XXV   Generate production / sales figures for location + material (under IS-OIL Traders Schedulers Workbench)

Generate production/sales figures for location + material

Production/sales object
Location
Material
Production version

Production/sales figures
Unit of measure
Forecast rack sales (issues)
Production quantity (receipts)

Date range
From date of generated data   09.01.2011
To date of generated data   09.01.2011

Update/delete control
⦿ Insert/update entries in DB
◯ Delete entries from DB

(ix)   Although we have not focused on the Financial and Accounting module, familiarise yourself with the module and how its different aspects, such as the postings into General Ledger, Accounts Payable, Accounts Receivable and Controlling, and Joint Venture Accounting, are connected to sales and billing in the SD module and Invoices raised in the MM module.

IV.IV Use the world-wide web (for example, www.google.com) as a starting point to investigate solutions; and if you are confused, to surf information on your task

Unlike the early days of SAP R/3, when there was little information available when you ran into difficulty on a project and your task, today, there are many blogs, forums, documents and information on the internet freely available to guide you; or give you some ideas on how to proceed; or how to deal with or approach a task in SAP R/3.

Hence, use the world-wide web (for example, www.google.com) as a starting point for solutions, or when you get confused or would like to know more concerning processes you are working on - surf the internet for further information on your task.

IV.V   Lessons from the Conglomerates and Transborder Corporations

In most conglomerates and transborder corporations, there will be a mixture of different SAP R/3 document types and records. For example, different SAP R/3 document types and records will interface within SD and logistic processes and FI. This will require a lot of testing of the business processes to certify that the solution architecture, design and development works.

It is not unlikely that you have a business process that starts with sales process (*Sales Activity > Inquiry > Quotation > Sales Order > Delivery > Billing > Accounting*), and then the conglomerate business also has the opportunity to service the equipment or product sold. This is not uncommon with conglomerates involved with the manufacturing of health care, electronics, oil and gas, pharmaceuticals and high-tech industries. The business process is: *Notification > Service Order > Billing*. When you now have to add purchase of spare parts (Materials Management module) and also service contract (a Sales Order document type) to this sales and service process, it gets more complicated. Once again, this will require a lot of testing of the business processes to certify that the solution architecture, design and development works.

A good starting point for fresh solutions in defining new business processes, or resolving issues and finding solutions may require using the world-wide web (for example, www.google.com) as a starting point for gathering information, if the required information is not readily available.

Chapter Five: Learn how to create Reports

One of the benefits of the SAP R/3 system is the ability to create reports that capture information across business processes useful to the business managers and stakeholders. As an SAP R/3 consultant you should be able to work with lists and create your own report using various tools in the standard SAP R/3 system. Business Intelligence Warehouse (BIW) is a client independent SAP R/3 module and advance reporting tool you may want to familiarise yourself with in the future for creating reports. BIW will take you where standard SAP R/3 will not go!

V.II Types of Reporting Tools

There are different ways you can create reports in an SAP R/3 system. In your early days as an SAP R/3 consultant you need to know how to retrieve some of these reports and how to work with them.

(i)   The first kind of reports you should know about are **Lists. Lists** are simple reports in the SAP R/3 system that you could easily retrieve using transaction codes and could also convert to various formats, including Microsoft excel. There are various types of lists, for example, lists of customers, lists of materials, lists of delivery, lists of billing documents etc.

An example of a list is shown below, using transaction code VA05: *Lists of Sales*

Figure V. I List of Sales

List of Sales Orders

List of Sales Orders

Sold-to party 0009413481
DITTA GIUSEPPE ZANZI & F
ROMA
Doc. Date   00.00.0000 To 10.05.2011

PO number	Doc. Date	Document	SaTy	Item	Sold-to pt	Material	Order qty	ConfirmQty	Batch	SU	Net	Curr.	Delivery date	Goods Issue	Description	Created by	RJ	Status
Trade	20.11.2002	184708	ZAS	10	9413481	4535630764...	1	1	U	PCE	0,00	EUR	21.11.2002	21.11.2002	2.5MHZ CWI PROB	IT14172		Completed
Trade	20.11.2002	184708	ZAS	10	9413481	4535630764...	1	0	U	PCE	0,00	EUR	20.11.2002	20.11.2002	2.5MHZ CWI PROB	IT14172		Completed
Trade	20.11.2002	184708	ZAS	11	9413481	4535630764...	1	0	D	PCE	0,00	EUR	20.11.2002	20.11.2002	2.5MHZ CWI PROB	ITSOGEMA2	90	Completed
prot 361	28.08.2002	84764	ZAS	10	9413481	4535632147...	1	0	U	PCE	0,00	EUR	28.08.2002	28.08.2002	Disk Dr. 3.5" floppy 1.44mb	IT14268		Completed
prot 361	28.08.2002	84764	ZAS	10	9413481	4535632147...	1	1	U	PCE	0,00	EUR	05.09.2002	05.09.2002	Disk Dr. 3.5" floppy 1.44mb	IT14268		Completed
ric. n.102/0...	23.08.2002	82449	ZAS	10	9413481	4535632992...	1	0	U	PCE	0,00	EUR	23.08.2002	23.08.2002	Power Supply Assy	IT14268		Completed
ric. n.102/0...	23.08.2002	82449	ZAS	10	9413481	4535632992...	1	1	U	PCE	0,00	EUR	27.08.2002	27.08.2002	Power Supply Assy	IT14268		Completed
3393101M	14.08.2002	77789	ZAS	10	9413481	4535630446...	1	1	U	PCE	0,00	EUR	20.08.2002	20.08.2002	UPS 240V 50/60 HZ	IT14268		Completed
3393101M	14.08.2002	77789	ZAS	10	9413481	4535630446...	1	0	U	PCE	0,00	EUR	14.08.2002	14.08.2002	UPS 240V 50/60 HZ	IT14268		Completed
3393101M	14.08.2002	77789	ZAS	20	9413481	4535632206...	1	0	U	PCE	0,00	EUR	14.08.2002	14.08.2002	MotherBd for VL400 (866mhz)	IT14268		Completed
3393101M	14.08.2002	77789	ZAS	20	9413481	4535632206...	1	1	U	PCE	0,00	EUR	20.08.2002	20.08.2002	MotherBd for VL400 (866mhz)	IT14268		Completed
3393101M	14.08.2002	77789	ZAS	30	9413481	4535632190...	1	0	U	PCE	0,00	EUR	14.08.2002	14.08.2002	HDD 6.4BG IDE 7200RPM 3.5	IT14268		Completed
3393101M	14.08.2002	77789	ZAS	30	9413481	4535632190...	1	1	U	PCE	0,00	EUR	20.08.2002	20.08.2002	HDD 6.4BG IDE 7200RPM 3.5	IT14268		Completed
3393101M	14.08.2002	77789	ZAS	40	9413481	4535632206...	1	0		PCE	0,00	EUR	14.08.2002	14.08.2002	MotherBdforVL400(866mhz)	EIJK	10	Completed
3393101M	14.08.2002	77789	ZAS	50	9413481	4535632190...	1	0		PCE	0,00	EUR	14.08.2002	14.08.2002	HDD6.4BGIDE7200RPM3.5	EIJK	10	Completed
3393101M	14.08.2002	77789	ZAS	60	9413481	4535630446...	1	0		PCE	0,00	EUR	14.08.2002	14.08.2002	UPS240V50/60HZ	EIJK	10	Completed

(ii)   There are **standard reporting programs** in the SAP R/3 that could meet your reporting requirements. There are thousands of reports in the SAP R/3 system (using transaction /nSA38) and we could activate them if they are not already being used.

(iii)   You could create your own specific report by making an **amendment to an SAP R/3 program.** However, modification of SAP R/3 codes is rarely done because of complications during upgrade of an SAP R/3 system.

(iv)   You could create **ABAP Queries**. This is done by using or creating User Groups, Functional Areas and Logical Database. We create a query with transactions SQ02, SQ03 and SQ00. A much quicker way of creating your query is to use the SAP R/3 tool called QuickViewer.

Figure V.II QuickViewer

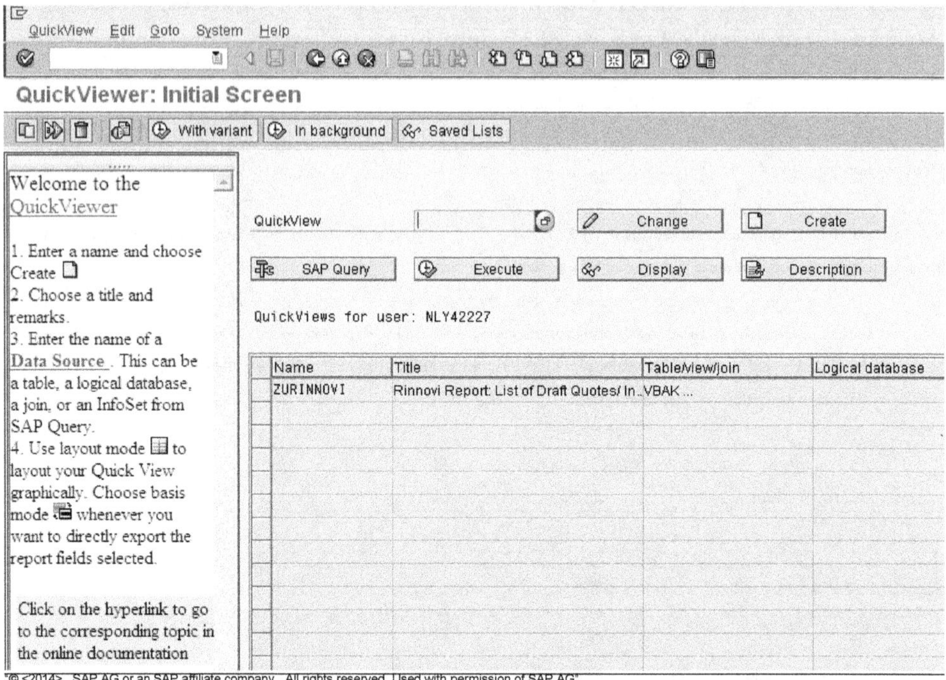

Figure V.III Selection Screen for Report titled Rinnovi Report (List of New Draft Quotes) run through transaction ZuRinnovi

Rinnovi Report

Sales Area	
Sales Organization	IT93
Distribution Channel	IT
Division	CS

Other selections			
Sales Group		to	
Sales Office		to	
Sales Document		to	
Quotation valid from		to	
Texts Including or Excluding	Y YE		

Figure V.IV The Report titled Rinnovi Report (with three tabs: Header data tab, Item data tab and Item Configuration tab)

Rinnovi Report

Header data | Item data | Item Config

Quote No	Item No	Sub-Item No	Equip. No	Techn. ID	Modality	System Code	System Desc.	Sold to Customer	Ship To Customer	Functional Location
10003511	1000		31180085		ULTRASOUND	PB016093	Ultrasound Syste...	ST.RADIOLOGICO DI FISCE...	AZIENDA OSPEDA...	IT000010-001-001
10003511	1000		31180086		ULTRASOUND	PB016092	NEO	ST.RADIOLOGICO DI FISCE...	AZIENDA OSPEDA...	IT000010-001-001
10003511	1000		31180118		ULTRASOUND	PB016048	Monitor - US	ST.RADIOLOGICO DI FISCE...	AZIENDA OSPEDA...	IT000010-001-001
10003511	1000		31180121		ULTRASOUND	PB016039	Application Softw...	ST.RADIOLOGICO DI FISCE...	AZIENDA OSPEDA...	IT000010-001-001
10003511	1000		31180122		ULTRASOUND	PB016040	Software Applicat...	ST.RADIOLOGICO DI FISCE...	AZIENDA OSPEDA...	IT000010-001-001
10003511	1000		32400234		ULTRASOUND	PB016092	NEO	ST.RADIOLOGICO DI FISCE...	AZIENDA OSPEDA...	IT000010-001-001
10003511	1000	1001	31180084			795052	iE33 Ultrasound ...	ST.RADIOLOGICO DI FISCE...	AZIENDA OSPEDA...	IT000010-001-001
10003511	1000	1999			ULTRASOUND			ST.RADIOLOGICO DI FISCE...	AZIENDA OSPEDA...	
10003511	1001	1002			ULTRASOUND			ST.RADIOLOGICO DI FISCE...	AZIENDA OSPEDA...	
10003512	1000				CMS			AZ.OSP.'OSP.SAN MARTINO'	AZ.OSP.'OSP.SAN ...	
10003512	1000	1001	11953053		CMS	989803110...	CodeMaster XL+ ...	AZ.OSP.'OSP.SAN MARTINO'	AZ.OSP.'OSP.SAN ...	IT000004-004-06
10003512	1000	1001	11953056		CMS	989803110...	CodeMaster XL+ ...	AZ.OSP.'OSP.SAN MARTINO'	AZ.OSP.'OSP.SAN ...	IT000004-004-06
10003512	1000	1002	11953050		CMS	989803110...	CodeMaster XL D...	AZ.OSP.'OSP.SAN MARTINO'	AZ.OSP.'OSP.SAN ...	IT000004-004-06

(v)   We have reporting tools such as **Report Writer** and **Report Painter**

(vi)   We also have **Logistic Information System** and **Sales Information System (LIS / SIS)** reporting tools which are made up of: Standard Analysis; Flexible Analysis; Early Warning Signal; Reporting Data (i.e. Standard Analysis data) in Excel (using Pivot table wizard, 3D column graphical representation).

We also have the Sales Information System **(SIS) Rebuild**.

(vii)   We can also create new **Information Structures** using transaction codes MC21 (Creating Info structure: Initial screen); OMOL (Standard Analysis: Initial Screen); MC24 (Creating Updating: Initial Screen)

(viii)   We can also create reports using Business Information Warehouse (BIW) / Data mining by designing Info Cubes. You should also learn to work with Excel sheets.

(ix)   Strategic Enterprise Management (SEM), an SAP R/3 module, could also provide necessary reports.

An SAP R/3 system is such a sophisticated tool you could manipulate it in different ways to create your desired reports. Good reports are required and are an important part of the justification for the need for an SAP R/3 modules integration.

Finally, for the reports to pick the necessary information, this will mean all SAP modules, for example SD, MM, FI/CO designed, integrated and implemented at one time have been properly customized, configured and activated, and records are inputted in time. It is your responsibility as a consultant to ensure that this is done for good reporting. Remember chapter four as we stated therein that you should familiarise yourself with different SAP R/3 document types and records indirectly related to SD and logistic process, as they could influence the success of your logistic module, processes, and project at hand - and now including the quality of your reporting.

<u>*V.III   Lessons from the Conglomerates and Transborder Corporations*</u>

The conglomerates and transborder corporations will run hundreds to thousands of various reports covering sales, customers, materials, spare parts, equipments, finance, accounting, costs, taxes, regulatory reports, FDA reports etc. This will not only be run on SAP R/3, but most times will also be downloaded onto Microsoft Excel sheets to be filtered and manipulated to give various results and pictures of the business.

For management, back office (IT skilled experts or an SAP R/3 Basis Consultant) may have to run these reports in the background or foreground, download them into Microsoft Excel and also automatically email them to management and users of such information for various business purposes.

It is therefore important for a new consultant to also know how to work with Microsoft Excel and manipulate information produced; run reports both in the background and in the foreground; and know how to distribute them to those who require such information.

Good reports drive decisions and profitability in conglomerates and transborder corporations.

Chapter Six: Understand Interfaces and how to work with third party softwares

<u>*VI.I Introduction*</u>

You need to understand and know the integration points between core SAP R/3 modules such as SD, MM, FI/CO, PS, PM and other applicable modules.

Also, you need to learn to understand the interfaces between SAP R/3 and third party softwares. These would generate what we call IDoc (meaning, *Intermediate document* which would encapsulate data so that it can be exchanged between different systems without conversion from one format to another). On some projects you may have to interface customer service softwares such as ServiceMax, Clarify, Adobe Flex or other third party CRM products to the Sales and Distribution module of an SAP R/3 system. You also need to understand the mapping of the different softwares and necessary tools to interface or make them work together. There are several ways of doing this. Sometimes this may only require enquiring from the manufacturer or the vendor of the third party software or SAP AG if there are already made tools to interface the two different products. This will require the ability to read programs, system messages and interprete them.

Furthermore, in technical terms, IDoc is a standard data structure for electronic data interchange (EDI) between application programs written for SAP R/3 or between an SAP application and an external program. IDocs serve as the vehicle for data transfer in SAP's Application Link Enabling (ALE) system. IDocs are used for asynchronous transactions: each IDoc generated exists as a self-contained text file that can then be transmitted to the requesting workstation without connecting to the central database. Another SAP mechanism, the Business Application Programming Interface (BAPI) is used for synchronous transactions. An IDoc encapsulates data so that it can be exchanged between different systems without conversion from one format to another. IDoc types define different categories of data or documents, which may then be broken down into more specific categories called *message types*. An IDoc can be generated at any point in a transaction and business process. For example, during a shipping transaction process, an IDoc may be generated that includes the data fields required to print a shipping manifest. After a user performs an SAP transaction, one or more IDocs are generated in the sending database and passed to the ALE communication layer. The communication layer performs a Remote Function Call (RFC), using the port definition and RFC destination specified by the customer model. The IDoc is transmitted to the receiver, which may be an SAP R/3, R/2, or some external system.

It is therefore important to understand interfaces and how to work with third party softwares.

<u>*VI.II General understanding of Interfaces*</u>

If you have third party software integrated with SAP R/3, then you will require interfaces that could be challenging at the early stages of design and testing. But once the systems stabilize it is usually okay.

At the early stages, when errors are generated between an SAP R/3 and the third party software, you will have to work on what we call the IDoc list to identify and resolve problems connected with these interfaces. An example of an IDOC list is shown below:

You input transaction WE02 in an SAP R/3 system, which gives you the IDOC list screen. In the screen you enter several parameters unique to the IDoc you are looking for, such as 'created at', 'created on' and other preferred selections before executing.

Figure VI.1 IDoc List

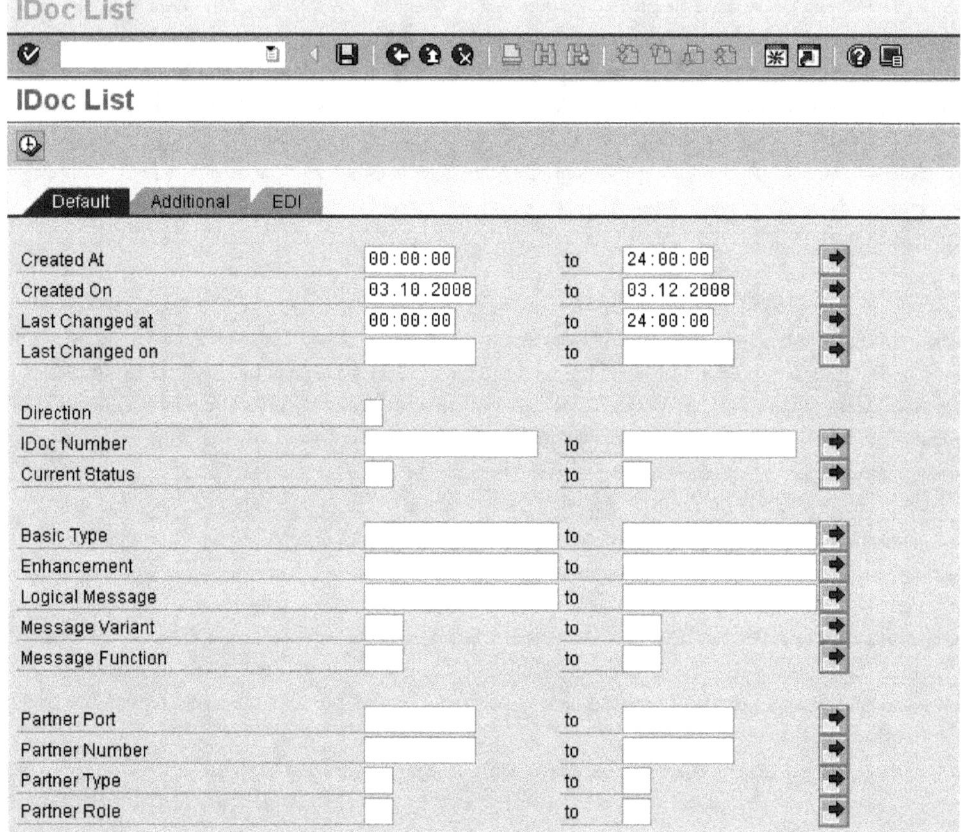

and then you have a list of IDocs based on your preferred selections.

Figure VI.II   Selected IDocs from IDoc List

IDocs	Numb
Selected IDocs	133265
▽ Outbound IDocs	023348
▷ ACLPAY	000087
▷ INVOIC	000538
▷ MBGMCR	000097
▷ RSINFO	019647
▷ RSSEND	000134
▷ YAMCOPAAC	000926
▷ YAM_IO16	000119
▷ YAM_IO11_IC	001800
▽ Inbound IDocs	109917
▷ CCLONE	000002
▷ COORP2	000001
▷ COND_A	009840
▷ CREMAS	000053
▷ CRESTA	001825
▷ DEBMAS	001825
▷ GLMAST	000001
▷ MATERIALVAI	003872
▷ MATMAS	048767
▷ MBGMCR	035490
▷ RSRQST	005319
▷ USERCLONE	000742
▷ YAMCOPAAC	000012
▷ YAMCOPAPL	000531
▷ YAM_IO10_IC	001637

Selected IDocs

IDoc Number	Segm	Stat	Stat	Partner	BasicType	Date created	Time	Messg.	Direction	Port
0000000006436616	53	03	○○□	LS/LS/SQ0CLNT5	INVOIC02	03.10.2008	01:25:46	INVOIC	Outbox	A000000002
0000000006436617	31	03	○○□	LS/ /SQ0CLNT500	YAMCOPAAC	03.10.2008	01:29:18	YAMCOP/	Outbox	A000000002
0000000006436618	1	03	○○□	LS/ /SQ0CLNT500	YAM_IO11_IC	03.10.2008	01:29:37	YAM_IO1	Outbox	A000000002
0000000006436619	2	53	○○□	LS/ /SQ5CLNT500	RSREQUST	03.10.2008	01:30:28	RSRQST	Inbox	SAPSQ5
0000000006436620	1	03	○○□	LS/ /SQ5CLNT500	RSINFO	03.10.2008	01:30:30	RSINFO	Outbox	A000000003
0000000006436621	1	03	○○□	LS/ /SQ5CLNT500	RSINFO	03.10.2008	01:30:30	RSINFO	Outbox	A000000003
0000000006436622	3	03	○○□	LS/ /SQ5CLNT500	RSINFO	03.10.2008	01:30:35	RSINFO	Outbox	A000000003
0000000006436623	1	03	○○□	LS/ /SQ5CLNT500	RSINFO	03.10.2008	01:30:35	RSINFO	Outbox	A000000003
0000000006436624	9	51	●○○	LS/ /SQ0500ARO	DEBMAS06	03.10.2008	01:36:56	DEBMAS	Inbox	SAPSQ0
0000000006436625	3	53	○○□	LS/ /SQ0500ARO	CRESTA01	03.10.2008	01:36:57	CRESTA	Inbox	SAPSQ0
0000000006436626	2	53	○○□	LS/ /SQ5CLNT500	RSREQUST	03.10.2008	03:01:30	RSRQST	Inbox	SAPSQ5
0000000006436627	1	03	○○□	LS/ /SQ5CLNT500	RSINFO	03.10.2008	03:01:31	RSINFO	Outbox	A000000003
0000000006436628	1	03	○○□	LS/ /SQ5CLNT500	RSINFO	03.10.2008	03:01:31	RSINFO	Outbox	A000000003
0000000006436629	2	03	○○□	LS/ /SQ5CLNT500	RSINFO	03.10.2008	03:01:33	RSINFO	Outbox	A000000003
0000000006436630	1	03	○○□	LS/ /SQ5CLNT500	RSINFO	03.10.2008	03:01:33	RSINFO	Outbox	A000000003
0000000006436631	2	53	○○□	LS/ /SQ5CLNT500	RSREQUST	03.10.2008	03:01:57	RSRQST	Inbox	SAPSQ5
0000000006436632	1	03	○○□	LS/ /SQ5CLNT500	RSINFO	03.10.2008	03:01:58	RSINFO	Outbox	A000000003
0000000006436633	1	03	○○□	LS/ /SQ5CLNT500	RSINFO	03.10.2008	03:01:58	RSINFO	Outbox	A000000003
0000000006436634	2	03	○○□	LS/ /SQ5CLNT500	RSINFO	03.10.2008	03:01:59	RSINFO	Outbox	A000000003
0000000006436635	1	03	○○□	LS/ /SQ5CLNT500	RSINFO	03.10.2008	03:01:59	RSINFO	Outbox	A000000003
0000000006436636	5	53	○○□	LS/ /SQ5CLNT500	RSREQUST	03.10.2008	03:02:23	RSRQST	Inbox	SAPSQ5
0000000006436637	1	03	○○□	LS/ /SQ5CLNT500	RSINFO	03.10.2008	03:02:24	RSINFO	Outbox	A000000003

Status Message for Selected IDoc

Status Text: IDoc: 0000000006436624 Status: Application document not posted

Error messages are usually highlighted by red lights meaning the outgoing or incoming information from an SAP R/3 has not been successful. In the example above, you can see an error message with status 51 with red coloured indicator meaning 'Error: Application document not posted'. You have to fix the error message for the incoming or outgoing information between the two softwares to be successful.

Figure VI.III   IDocs Display

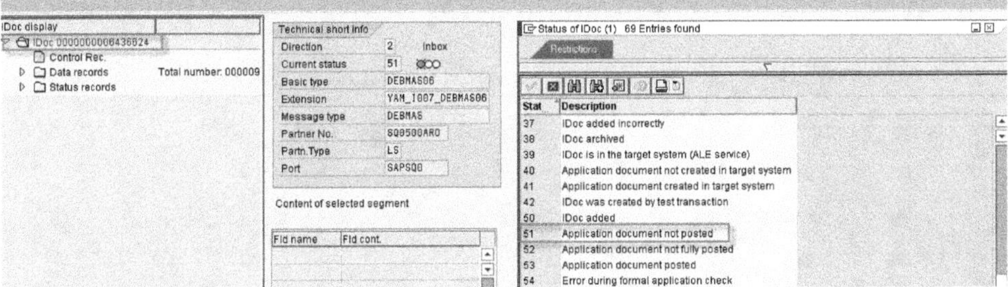

To process IDoc messages you will require transaction codes such as WE19, BDM2 and BD87 to resolve message types.

Figure VI.IV   Test tool for IDoc processing (WE19)

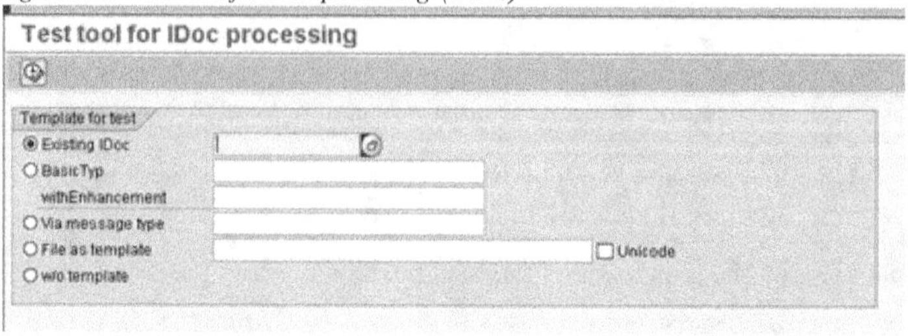

Figure VI.V   IDoc Trace (BDM2)

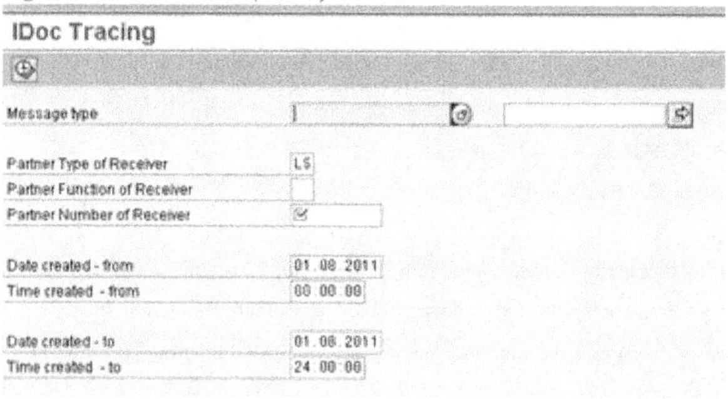

IDoc processing using IDoc trace based on Message type(s) as selection criteria on the entry screen.

Figure VI. VI Select IDocs (BD87)

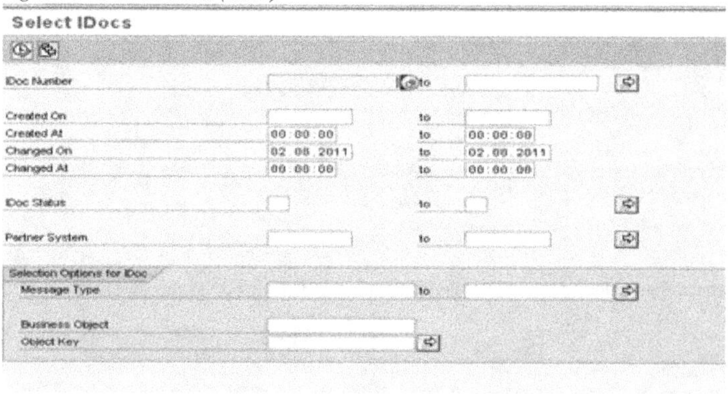

Figure VI. VII Status Monitor for ALE Messages (BD87)

Status Monitor for ALE Messages

Docs	IDoc Status	Number
▽ ▼ IDoc selection		
▼ IDoc Number is equal to 446825562		
▼ Changed on is in the range 02.08.2011 to 02.08.2011		
▽ ⬛ RR1 Client 500		1
▽ ⬛ IDoc in inbound processing		1
▷ ▢ Application document posted	53	1

Status 53 (Application posted successfully) for an IDoc number that is successful.

VI.III General understanding of an SAP business defined entry screen

Also, it is required that you are aware of an SAP R/3 business defined entry screen. Sometimes for the purposes of customer service or customer relationship management, a business may decide to create a more user-friendly entry screen using an SAP R/3 programming language ABAP to create this entry screen.

Also, you will frequently come across situations whereby standard SAP R/3 reports and documents will also have to be redefined (usually we use the term 'enhanced' or 'enhancement') to meet a particular business criteria when, as is standard, SAP R/3 reports and documents will not meet business specific requirements.

A more elementary situation will be working with 'list' and tweaking the document by deleting or adding various fields and elements to meet a particular business requirement. We will use the term working with *variants* in this case.

VI.IV General understanding of SAP Business Intelligence

What a standard SAP R/3 system reporting tool will not do, an SAP Business Intelligence will achieve. It is particularly useful in creating reports that cut across various SAP R/3 modules, which may not be easily achieved in the SAP R/3 system. SAP Business Intelligence is commonly used with a standard SAP R/3 system. The two systems are client independent, that is, when used together in the same business, they exist on separate independent clients.

An SAP R/3 Business Intelligence system could also work as a standalone system, and could also be interfaced with other third party softwares and not only with an SAP R/3 system.

VI.V General understanding of SAP CRM

What a standard SAP R/3 system will not achieve in terms of sales relationship (inquiries, quotation creation and sales ordering and management) and customer after-sales relationship (customer service), an SAP R/3 Customer Relationship Management (CRM) will achieve.

SAP CRM is commonly used with a standard SAP R/3 system. The two systems are client independent, that is, when used together in the same business, they exist on separate independent clients.

An SAP R/3 CRM system could also work as a standalone system, and could also be interfaced with other third party softwares and not only with an SAP R/3 system.

VI.VI General understanding of third party software such as ServiceMax, Clarify, Mobile Solution, Adobe Flex etc.

Working as an SAP R/3 consultant you also need to have a general understanding of third party softwares such as Clarify, FLEX, Siebel, Mobile Solution softwares and how they are used and interfaced with SAP R/3 in the logistics area.

You must also be aware that various industries using SAP R/3 will also use other third party softwares to perform certain activities and processes that they believe an SAP R/3 will not do or give them optimum value. Hence, they will want to interface SAP R/3 with such activities and processes done in other third party softwares. For example, the oil and gas industry is very complex, risky and litigious. While most of the biggest global oil and gas companies usually called 'the seven sisters' use SAP R/3 to manage their value chain (*Exploration > Development > Production > Trading > Transport > Refining > Retail*), along the process chain are hundreds of other smaller third party softwares interfaced with SAP R/3 or that operate as standalones alongside an SAP R/3.

In the customer service functional area, you will find softwares such as ServiceMax, Clarify and Mobile Solution interfaced with an SAP R/3 system.

In the Sales and Distribution and Customer Service area of SAP R/3, FLEX software may be used as the front end for the core processes of Customer Sales such as Sales Activity > Inquiry > Quotation > Sales Order > Billing.

VI.VII   Lessons from the Conglomerates and Transborder Corporations

A lot of conglomerates and transborder corporations will primarily use an SAP R/3 system to manage their value chain, and along the process chain could be other smaller third party softwares interfaced with SAP R/3 or that operate as standalones alongside an SAP R/3.

Chapter Seven: Adaptation of SAP Development Objects and how the SAP Enhancement Framework is used

VII.I Regularly use Help (F1) to retrieve information about SAP R/3 Tables and Fields

By pressing **F1** on your personal computer keyboard on a field, you can find the technical information for that field and document (for example, table, fields, data elements and program name). For example, in a sales document, by pressing F1 on the field 'Standard Order', the technical information gives you the table name VBAK and other technical information. That technical information you can input in the data dictionary to display all information on all sales documents and fields you want to investigate in the system. You can use VBAK to produce a list of sales documents in the system.

Figure VII.I   Using F1 (Help) to retrieve Technical Information

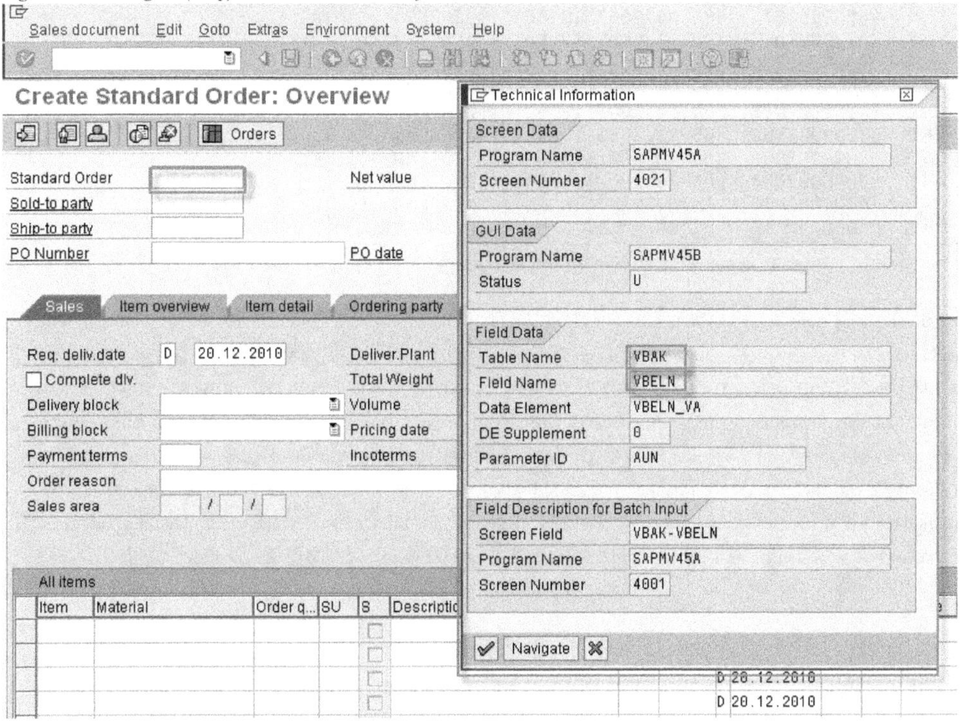

VII.II The data dictionary and working with tables and fields

Technically, using transaction **SE16**, input VBAK in the table field, you can produce a list of sales documents already created and saved in the SAP R/3 system. In Figure VII.I, we are able to produce a list of sales documents which gives information about the following: MANDT (Client); VBELN (the number that uniquely identifies the sales document); ERDAT (Date on which the record was created); and ERNAM (Name of person who created the object).

Figure VII.II   Using the Data Browser to retrieve further Information (SE16)

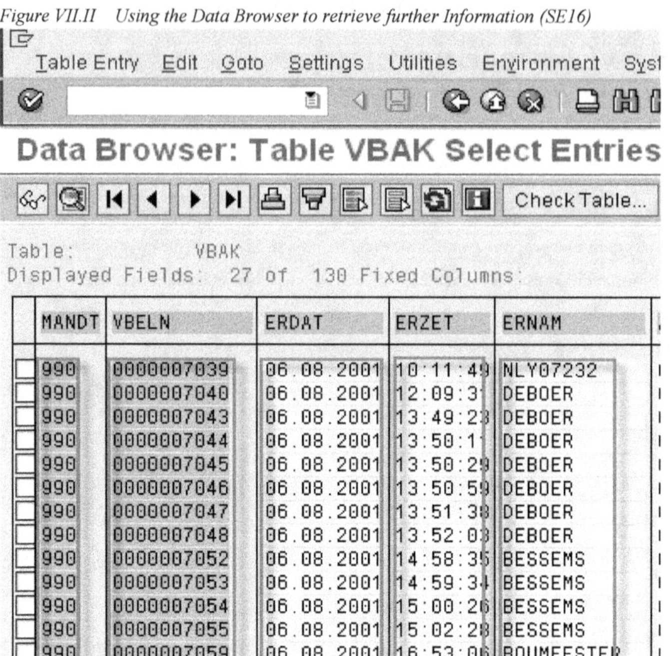

MANDT	VBELN	ERDAT	ERZET	ERNAM	
990	0000007039	06.08.2001	10:11:49	NLY07232	
990	0000007040	06.08.2001	12:09:3	DEBOER	
990	0000007043	06.08.2001	13:49:23	DEBOER	
990	0000007044	06.08.2001	13:50:1	DEBOER	
990	0000007045	06.08.2001	13:50:29	DEBOER	
990	0000007046	06.08.2001	13:50:59	DEBOER	
990	0000007047	06.08.2001	13:51:38	DEBOER	
990	0000007048	06.08.2001	13:52:03	DEBOER	
990	0000007052	06.08.2001	14:58:35	BESSEMS	
990	0000007053	06.08.2001	14:59:34	BESSEMS	
990	0000007054	06.08.2001	15:00:26	BESSEMS	
990	0000007055	06.08.2001	15:02:28	BESSEMS	
990	0000007059	06.08.2001	16:53:06	BOUMEESTER	

Alternatively, using transaction **SE16n** to search for lists of sales documents, it even gets much clearer. You can find further technical data for the sales documents header data created in the system. For example, MANDT, VBELN, ERDAT, ERZET, ERNAM, ANGOT, BNDDT, AUDAT, VBTYP, TRVOG, AUART, AUGRU, GWLDT, SUBMI, LIFSK, FAKSK, NETWR, WAERK, VKORG, VTWEG, SPART, VKGRP. You can use any of these technical field names to carry out further searches in the system concerning sales document header data information. You can use them to produce specific lists and reports for each field name. For example, you could find out lists of sales documents (VBELN) by drilling down. You could find out list of sales document created by 'EXLIET' (ERNAM) by drilling down. You could find out the number of a select number of sales documents using the valid from (ANGOT) and the valid to (BNDDT) field names by drilling down.

Figure VII.III   General Table Display **(SE16n)**

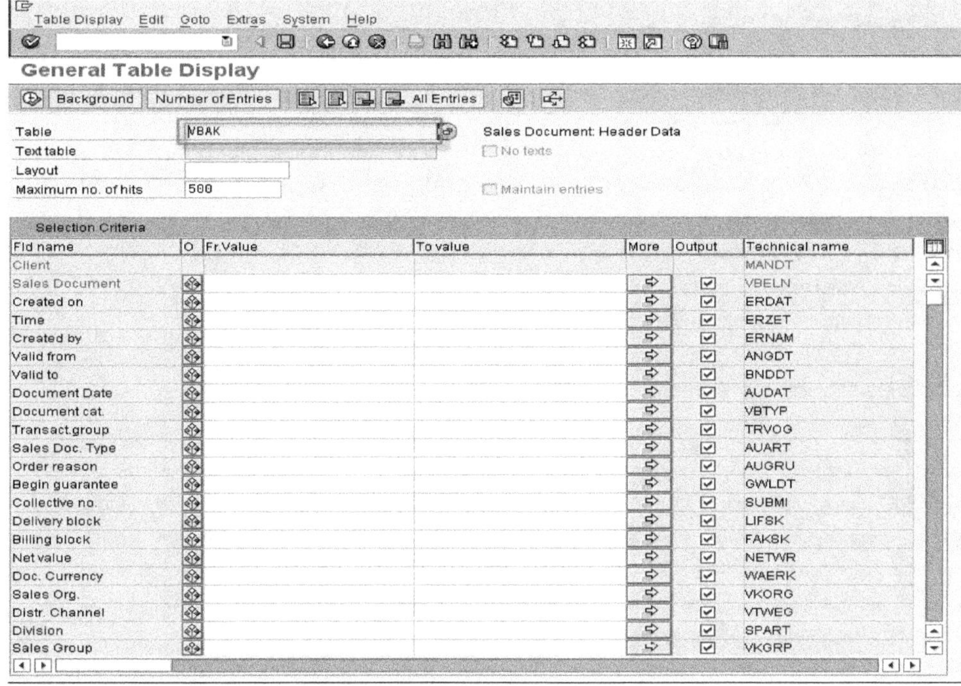

And all entries are displayed.

Figure VII.IV   Display of Table Entries Found **(SE16n)**

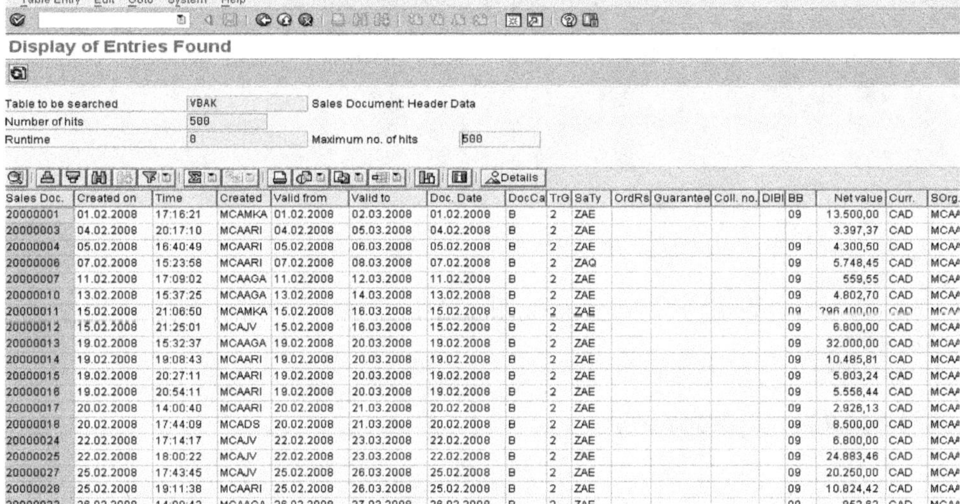

Sales Doc.	Created on	Time	Created	Valid from	Valid to	Doc. Date	DocCa	TrG	SaTy	OrdRs	Guarantee	Coll. no.	DIBl	BB	Net value	Curr.	SOrg.
20000001	01.02.2008	17:16:21	MCAMKA	01.02.2008	02.03.2008	01.02.2008	B	2	ZAE					09	13.500,00	CAD	MCA?
20000003	04.02.2008	20:17:10	MCAARI	04.02.2008	05.03.2008	04.02.2008	B	2	ZAE						3.397,37	CAD	MCA?
20000004	05.02.2008	16:40:49	MCAARI	05.02.2008	06.03.2008	05.02.2008	B	2	ZAE					09	4.300,50	CAD	MCA?
20000006	07.02.2008	15:23:58	MCAARI	07.02.2008	08.03.2008	07.02.2008	B	2	ZAQ					09	5.748,45	CAD	MCA?
20000007	11.02.2008	17:09:02	MCAAGA	11.02.2008	12.03.2008	11.02.2008	B	2	ZAE					09	559,55	CAD	MCA?
20000010	13.02.2008	15:37:25	MCAAGA	13.02.2008	14.03.2008	13.02.2008	B	2	ZAE					09	4.802,70	CAD	MCA?
20000011	15.02.2008	21:06:50	MCAMKA	15.02.2008	16.03.2008	15.02.2008	B	2	ZAE					09	796.400,00	CAD	MCA?
20000012	15.02.2008	21:25:01	MCAJV	15.02.2008	16.03.2008	15.02.2008	B	2	ZAE					09	6.800,00	CAD	MCA?
20000013	19.02.2008	15:32:37	MCAAGA	19.02.2008	20.03.2008	19.02.2008	B	2	ZAE					09	32.000,00	CAD	MCA?
20000014	19.02.2008	19:08:43	MCAARI	19.02.2008	20.03.2008	19.02.2008	B	2	ZAE					09	10.485,81	CAD	MCA?
20000015	19.02.2008	20:27:11	MCAARI	19.02.2008	20.03.2008	19.02.2008	B	2	ZAE					09	5.803,24	CAD	MCA?
20000016	19.02.2008	20:54:11	MCAARI	19.02.2008	20.03.2008	19.02.2008	B	2	ZAE					09	5.556,44	CAD	MCA?
20000017	20.02.2008	14:00:40	MCAARI	20.02.2008	21.03.2008	20.02.2008	B	2	ZAE					09	2.926,13	CAD	MCA?
20000018	20.02.2008	17:44:09	MCADS	20.02.2008	21.03.2008	20.02.2008	B	2	ZAE					09	8.500,00	CAD	MCA?
20000024	22.02.2008	17:14:17	MCAJV	22.02.2008	23.03.2008	22.02.2008	B	2	ZAE					09	6.800,00	CAD	MCA?
20000025	22.02.2008	18:00:22	MCAJV	22.02.2008	23.03.2008	22.02.2008	B	2	ZAE					09	24.883,46	CAD	MCA?
20000027	25.02.2008	17:43:45	MCAJV	25.02.2008	26.03.2008	25.02.2008	B	2	ZAE					09	20.250,00	CAD	MCA?
20000028	25.02.2008	19:11:38	MCAARI	25.02.2008	26.03.2008	25.02.2008	B	2	ZAE					09	10.824,42	CAD	MCA?
20000032	26.02.2008	14:00:43	MCAAGA	26.02.2008	27.03.2008	26.02.2008	B	2	ZAE					09	952,82	CAD	MCA?

You can also select and deselect field names in your searches for better search outputs.

VII.III Maintain Table by Debugging

Go to SE16 and display table to be maintained, if we have a custom table.

Next step, you click on a line to copy and display. Once the table is displayed, you type /n in the transaction box and click enter twice. Now you enter the Debug mode; if code = 'SHOW' ; look at the lower box, make value (VAL) is also showing SHOW click on change button and type INSR (if you want to insert); DELE (if you want to delete); EDIT (if you want to edit). Then click enter and execute using the symbol with the arrow pointing down.

You can now insert in the table your new parameter and other entries applicable. Then click enter and save.

Then 'Database record successfully created' appears below.

Then go back to refresh table to see new entries.

VII. IV Working with enhancements / user exits (CMOD)

Used in cases whereby standard SAP R/3 objects will have to be redefined (usually we use the term 'enhanced') to meet a particular business criteria when as-is standard SAP R/3 objects will not meet business specific requirements. The basic idea of an SAP R/3 Enhancements and Framework is to make modification-free enhancements of development objects such as programs, function modules, tables / structures, global classes, and Web Dynpro components. The basic concept is the enhancement option and think of it as a hook on which you can attach the enhancement implementation elements to. If an SAP system provides these hooks, you can add an implementation element there at later stages of development in other systems, without modifying the original SAP code.

Using transaction **CMOD**, for User Exits, you select your user exit: YAM_E001 and find out where you can assign this user exit / enhancement.

Figure VII.V   SAP Enhancements

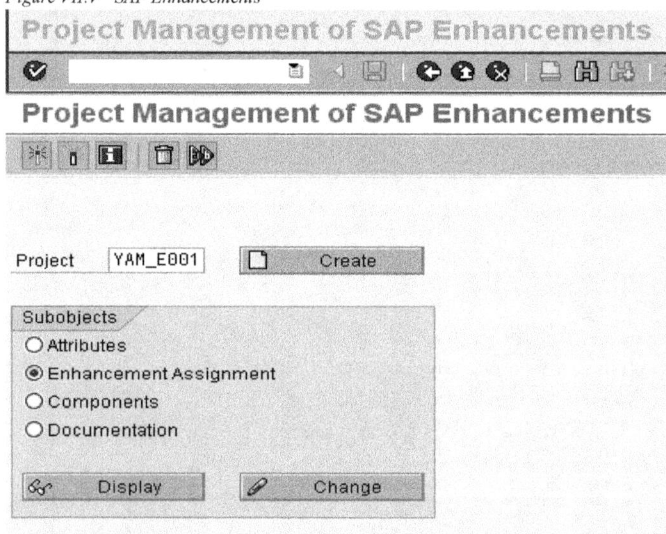

Click on Enhancement Assignments and Display, and you get the following screen telling you where you can use the user exit / enhancement in resource-related billing and quotation creation, and that you can use them to complete item fields and add further partners to the item, when you create the item.

Figure VII.VI SAP Enhancements (II)

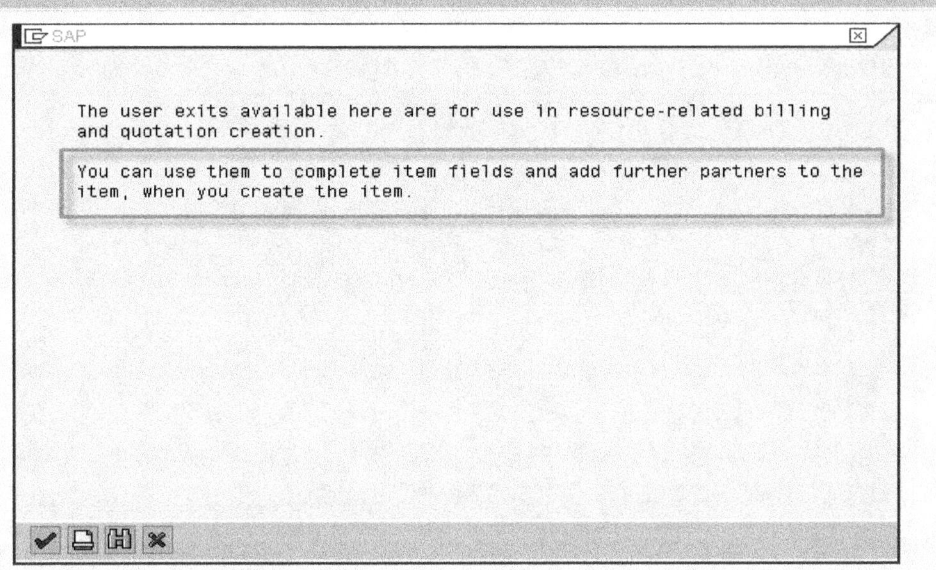

Now you can see the function exits within the enhancement itself.

Figure VII.VII SAP Enhancements Assignments

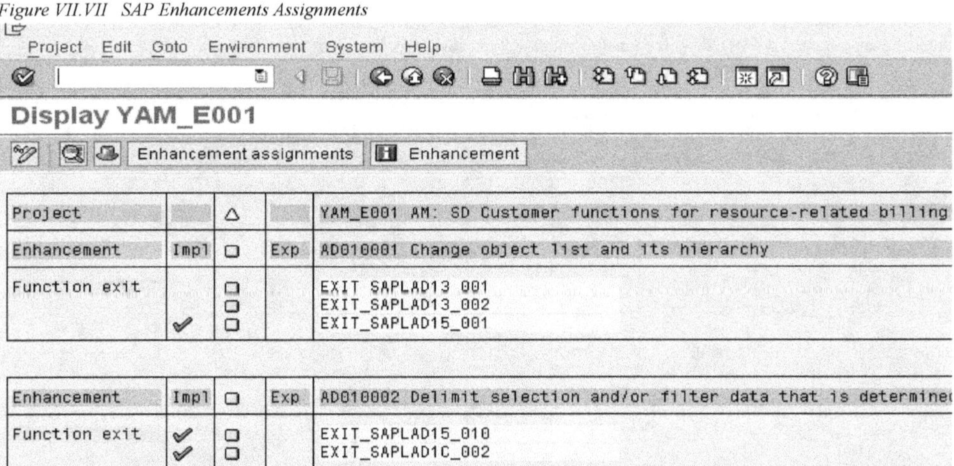

Double click on the exit. Now the function module EXIT_SAPLAD13_001_001 is displayed.

Figure VII.VIII   SAP Enhancements – Function Module Displayed

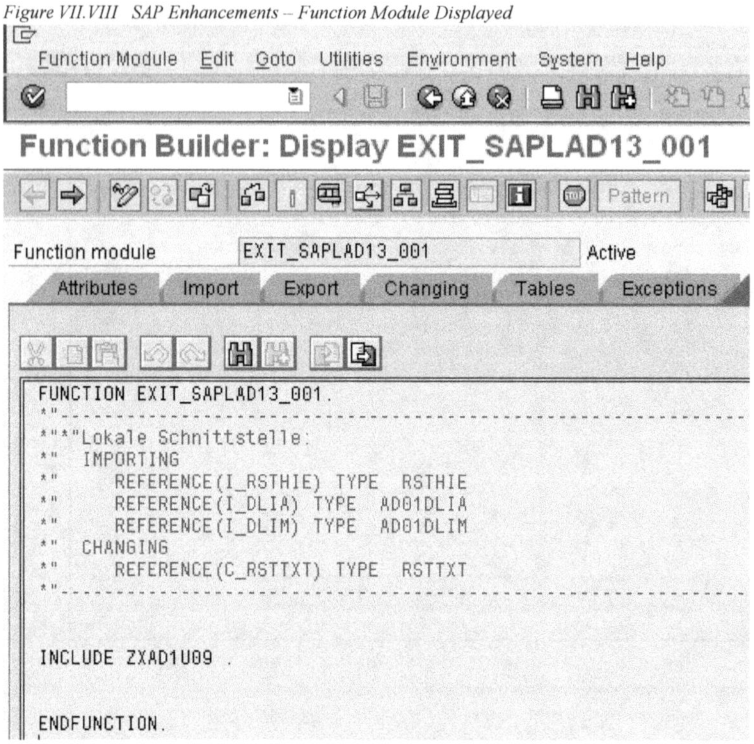

Double click on Include ZXAD1U09 in the function module. Insert the 'code or coding' into the Include ZXAD1U09:

Figure VII.IX   SAP Enhancements – Function Module Displayed (II)

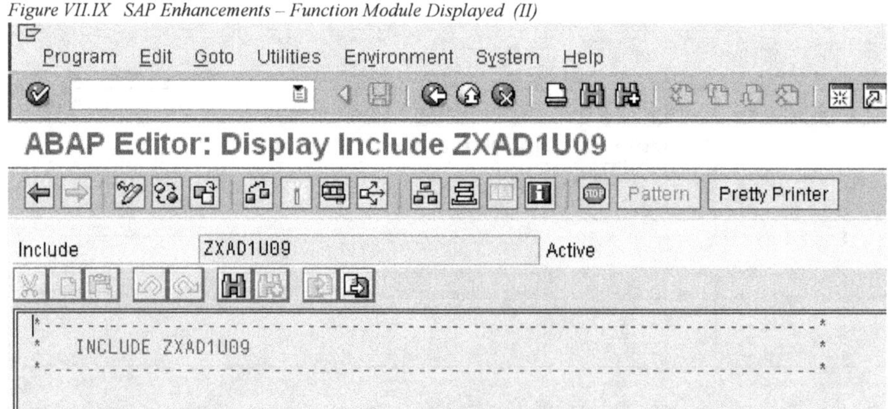

Activate the Include program ZXAD1U09. Go back to CMOD and activate the project. This is one of many other ways you can work with enhancements / user exits in your program.

There is also transaction code **SMOD** which gives you a list of enhancements in the system.

VII.V SAP Business Workflow

SAP Business Workflow can be used to define business processes. These may be simple release or approval procedures. It is particularly suitable for situations in which work processes have to be run through repeatedly, or situations in which the business process requires the involvement of a large number of agents in a specific sequence.

VII.VI Data Archiving

Archiving is used to store old data, using the *Archive Data Kit* (ADK). Key transaction code is: SARA

Assuming we were in the process of archiving old purchase orders, from transaction code ME23n we should be able to read from Optical Archive, for example, 'Purchase Order has been archived and data can be displayed'.

VII.VII Lessons from the Conglomerates and Transborder Corporations

Complex organisations will have several adaptations of SAP development objects to achieve optimal efficiency of their business processes. There would be several enhancement of SAP development objects; function modules; usage of SAP Business Workflow; and Data Archiving in complex organisations.

Chapter Eight: Security and Authorization

VIII.I You can assign security and authorization to organisations

Using transaction S_BCE_68001425, you can track the authorization objects related to various organisations.

For example, you will have authorization objects such as V_VBAK_VKO, which is described as Sales Document authorization for Sales Area. If security and authorization is restricted to this, access to this level of authorization could mean users could create, change and display sales documents within this entire sales area.

Figure VIII.I: Selection Criteria for Authorization by Organisation

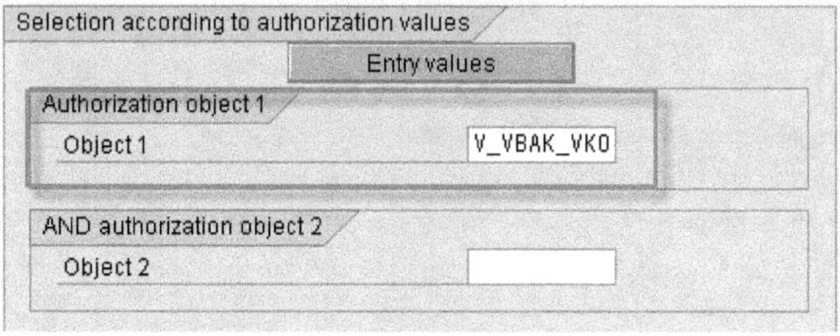

VIII.II You can assign security and authorization to documents or transactions assigned in SAP menu

You can track the authorization objects related to documents or transactions assigned in SAP menu within your functional area.

For example, having authorization object V_VBAK_VKO with another authorization object such as V_VBAK_AAT, which is described as the Sales Document Authorization for Sales Document Types, could mean specific users or user groups may be prevented or given access to various or specific sales document types within a specific sales area. Further restriction by limiting a user to a specific transaction code (for example, VA13) could mean such a user would only have access to that specific transaction code.

Figure VIII.II: Selection Criteria for Authorization by documents and transaction codes

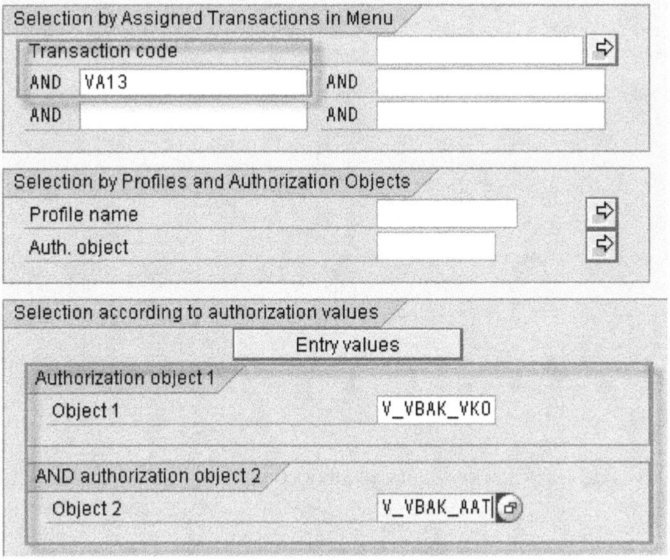

VIII.III You can assign security and authorization in business parameters (such as cost centres, plants, personnel area, controlling area etc.) within function modules

Security and Authorization team or consultant can set authorization checks within function modules to prevent users from accessing unauthorised important company, business partners, cost centres, plants, controlling area and personnel data information. However, for specific users, this authorization check could be bypassed by fetching data from tables instead of using specific restrictive function modules.

For example, for customer sales and service, as we are having authorization objects V_VBAK_VKO (Sales Document Authorization for Sales Area) and V_VBAK_AAT (Sales Document Authorization for Sales Document Types) already. We may also use function modules SD_KOMV_ARRAY_SELECT (Pricing conditions) and VC_I_GET_CONFIGURATION (Configuration details) for further security and restrictions. Hovever, the usage of function modules such as EQUIPMENT_READ (Equipment details) and PM_HIERARCHY_CALL (Equipment Hierarchy details) can be omitted to avoid restrictions that may be applicable to cost centres and plant maintenance business parameters already set in the function modules company wide. Instead, information could be fetched from tables to avoid cost centres and plant maintenance authorization checks and restrictions within the two function modules EQUIPMENT _READ (Equipment details) and PM_HIERARCHY_CALL (Equipment Hierarchy details).

VIII.IV   You can assign security and authorization to users

If you have SAP R/3 user IDs set up (for example, EXTLIET); individual users could have transaction codes or SAP R/3 roles linked to their user IDs.

Figure VIII.III: Selection Criteria for Authorization by user IDs

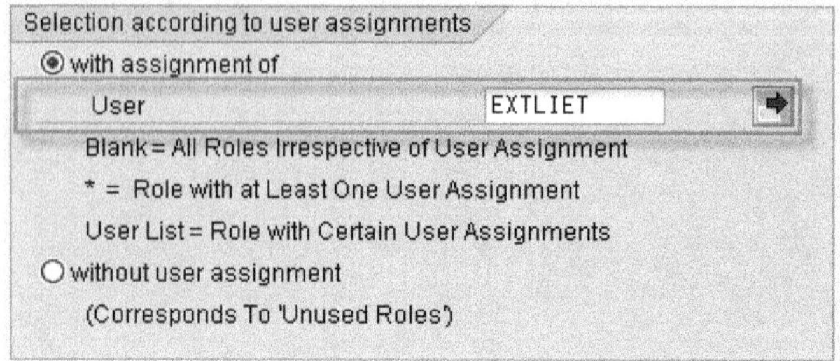

For example through the user ID EXTLIET, you can find all the roles linked to user ID EXTLIET.

Figure VIII IV: User specific ID linked to roles

Roles found

TRITD.PMATR		IT : Materials Reporting
TRITD.PPURR		IT : Purchasing Reporting
TRITD.QARCR		IT : Accounts Receivable Reporting
TRITD.QSALR		IT : Sales Reporting
TRITD.QSRVMR		IT : Service Management Reporting
TRITD.RFICOR		IT : FiCo Reporting
TRITA.QMCORA		IT : Maintain Contracts & Rebate Agreements
TRITA.QMINQ		IT : Maintain Inquiries
TRITA.QMSACT		IT : Maintain Sales Activities
TRITA.QMSCON		IT : Maintain Sales Conditions

VIII. V   You can assign security and authorization to SAP Roles

Generally user IDs and applicable transaction codes for specific users will be mapped to SAP R/3 roles. For example, user ID EXTLIET that require a report based on Create and Change of Inquiries (VA01 and VA02) could be linked to SAP role TRITA.QMINQ (that is, IT: Maintain Inquiries) and if Display of List of Inquiries is also required, could also be linked to TRITD.QSALR (IT: Sales Reporting).

Figure VIII.V: Selection Criteria for Authorization by SAP Roles

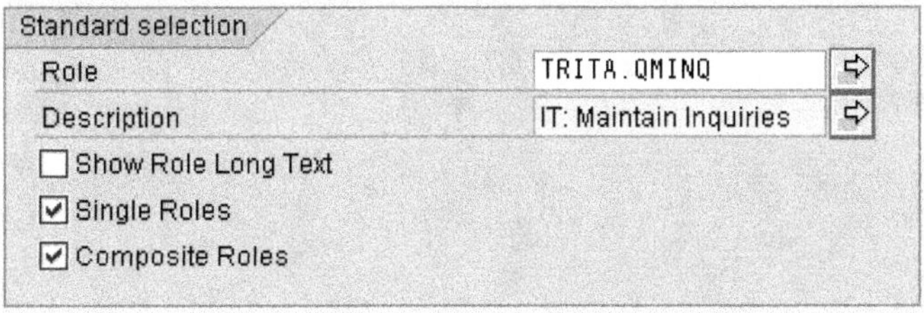

Standard selection		
Role	TRITA.QMINQ	⇨
Description	IT: Maintain Inquiries	⇨
☐ Show Role Long Text		
☑ Single Roles		
☑ Composite Roles		

VIII. VI   Lessons from the Conglomerates and Transborder Corporations

With most conglomerates and transborder corporations, security and authorization will be role based and not specific to users.

Generally, conglomerates will manage their security and authorization through a varied combination of complex criteria that will include role based mapping.

Figure VIII.VI: Security and Authorization via Role based complex selection criteria

Roles by Complex Selection Criteria

Standard selection

Role	TRITA.QMINQ
Description	IT: Maintain Inquiries

☐ Show Role Long Text
☑ Single Roles
☑ Composite Roles

Selection according to user assignments

◉ with assignment of

User	EXTLIET

Blank = All Roles Irrespective of User Assignment

* = Role with at Least One User Assignment

User List = Role with Certain User Assignments

○ without user assignment

(Corresponds To 'Unused Roles')

Selection by Assigned Transactions in Menu

Transaction code

AND	VA13	AND	
AND		AND	

Selection by Profiles and Authorization Objects

Profile name	
Auth. object	

Selection according to authorization values

Entry values

Authorization object 1

Object 1	V_VBAK_VKO

AND authorization object 2

Object 2	V_VBAK_AAT

Chapter Nine: Project Management of an SAP R/3 environment

IX.I Get your team set up right (i.e. know strengths and weaknesses)

As a new SAP R/3 consultant I do not expect you to be a project manager on day one.

But I have experienced many times on SAP R/3 projects many project managers who have no clue of an SAP R/3 system and what it looks like. Some are even very arrogant and this is very risky. As a result their decisions are not based on best practice, reason and knowledge, but on who has the best communication skills. In situations like this, best decisions are rarely made. If you are such a project manager you need to read this book, particularly the earlier chapters, to have a general idea of SAP R/3, as well as this chapter and the following chapters. I always wonder why take a big risk on a complex SAP R/3 system with a project manager that has no basic understanding of the functional and technical design and methodology of an SAP R/3 system.

If you happen to be a project manager without SAP R/3 system knowledge and hands-on skill set, you need to set up your team right. Foremost, you will need by your side someone with sound technical know-how, solution architecture and integration knowledge to help with your project, and identify good functional and technical consultants, and team leaders. I have played the role of Solution Architect and Integration Manager (technical hands-on) to support such project managers without any SAP R/3 knowledge.

Particularly on major global projects, as a new SAP R/3 project manager / consultant you should have a cultural and racial mix of resources and personnel. Learn to speak loud and clearly. Do not be biased culturally in your views. Learn the basics of teamwork working with various races, cultures and countries. It is important that you understand what is important to various businesses from the perspective of their people, culture and society. If you are from Western Europe and you are going to work in China, India, Africa, South America, you have much learning to do in terms of cultures and your expectations; the value systems abroad are just different from yours. In some societies decisions are made based on general consensus and in others it is based on seniority of ranks or age. Once the leader gives the nod, the rest of the business personnel follow the leader(s) direction. This is just culture.

Also know the strengths and weaknesses of your team.

You as an SAP R/3 project manager should be a thinker and should surround yourself with thinkers! Serious thinking and planning are what you must do when designing solutions for complex organisations! And also note every project is different.

IX. II Be clear about the stakeholders' objectives

As a new SAP R/3 project manager / consultant be clear about the stakeholders' objectives. There are many projects without management buy-in and committed stakeholders. This is usually because business managers are not clear on what to expect during the process of system design and implementation. There is no point managing a project without any or much support from the business and project stakeholders. It is important you have a project methodology well defined and change management processes, so as to carry the business and project team along the SAP R/3 project cycle and roadmap (that is, *ASAP Roadmap Methodology: Project Preparation > Business Blueprint > Realisation > Final Preparation > Go-Live and Support*). If you are able to carry the business, the stakeholders and project team along, you therefore create a win-win situation for your project and the business about to have a new business system. The probability of your success is indeed much higher.

IX. III   Communicate early SAP R/3 benefits

Communicate with both your team and the business through sound project and change management processes using an SAP R/3 methodology roadmap. Set daily, weekly and monthly targets and timelines. Address difficulties and they should be faced head-on and resolved. Communicate, communicate and communicate, there is no other way. Although you also need to be aware that in some cultures decision-making through communication is only through the senior ranking leaders.

IX. IV   Communicate early what will not be realised within this phase of the project and budget

Early in the project you must clarify, establish and communicate the scope of your project (for each particular phase) to avoid 'scope creep'. Some global corporations have on-going SAP R/3 projects, therefore have several project phases and overlapping projects. Sometimes these projects are three to six months per cycle for each new project. You do not want new demands and requirements creeping into your project at later stages; you may have big problems on your hands.

It is also important that while you are making decisions in terms of resources (staffing), SAP R/3 process demands and requirements to be realised in your project, you also need to be in control of the financial budget and come out with a profit at the end of your project. Therefore, you will need an adequate project management toolkit and training to manage the planning and cost side of your project to come out with profit. The *Project Management Institute* (PMI) training and Project *Management Professional* (PMP) certification could be helpful.

IX. V   Set realistic timelines
As a new SAP R/3 project manager / consultant, set realistic timelines for your project. For you to be able to set realistic timelines realistically, you must know something about an SAP R/3 system, have competent consultants and be aware of your budget restrictions. It is only on the basis of this that you can set realistic timelines for your project.

IX. VI   Use ASAP Methodology, Solution Manager and other project management tools

Use ASAP Methodology, Solution Manager and other project management tools

IX. VII   Lessons from the Conglomerates and Transborder Corporations

Complex organisations such as conglomerates and transborder corporations will require well detailed planning of projects, tested tools and methodologies for projects to succeed.

Chapter Ten: Continuous Training

X. I   Importance of continuous training

The best way to learn and improve your technical skills in a fast changing technological world is to embark on continuous training. You can never substitute the benefits of good and continuous training.

X. II   Three level strategy for successful training

As a new SAP R/3 project manager / consultant, to increase the heights and depths of your own training and your project team, you must establish excellent training conditions (that is, create an excellent training environment; get quality trainers; and you and your team must have the right attitude to training). At the core of this exercise must be continuous training review, further development and 'the doers' training.

Train the key business users and project management team from basic things to complex configuration depending on work tasks and security authorizations. For example, training of general users will centre on how to logon, use of F1/ F2, /n, /o, setting up Area Menus & User Parameters.

You must train executives and business managers how to get their reports and key figures out, and how to derive business benefits from the data using ABAP Query, Logistic / Sales Information System (LIS/SIS), Pricing Reports and Analysis, Different Outputs types and forms.

The requirement for training will also be important for Business Development Executives, Accountants and Auditors, Supply Chain Managers, Corporate Financiers (Investment Bankers), Legal Specialists involved in Mergers and Acquisitions and SAP R/3 legal validation, and other specialists and professionals also, directly and indirectly, involved in cross border and transnational transactions and those areas that conglomerates cut across.

Figure X.I: Three level strategy for successful training

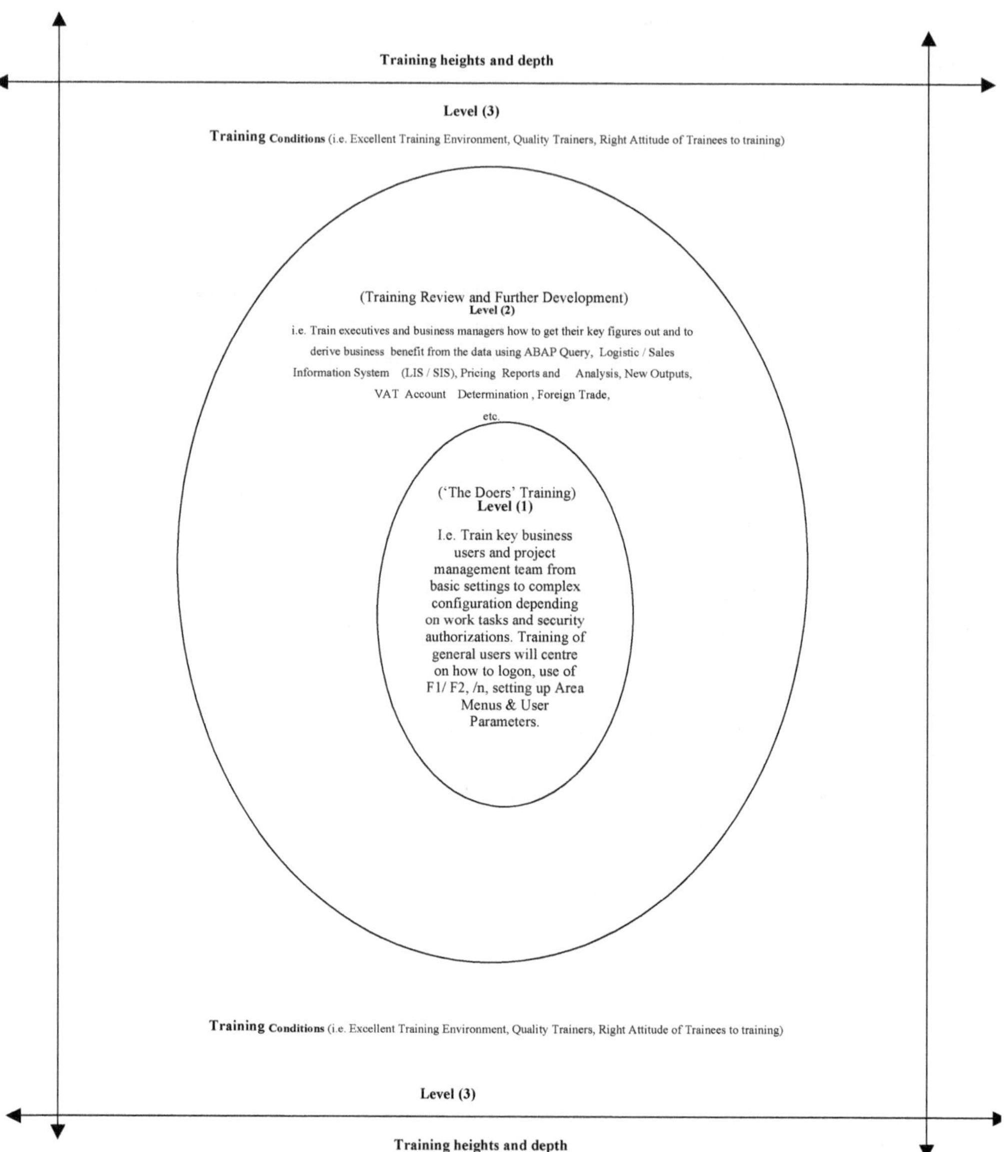

Copyright. Lionel Etan-Adollo (2014)

<u>Level (1) - Train the key business users and project management team from basic settings to complex configurations depending on work tasks and security authorizations:</u>

- This is the first level and what I term 'The Doers' training.
- Key business users, super users and project management members are trained from basic settings to complex configurations depending on work tasks and security authorizations.
- Training of general users will centre on how to logon, use of F1/ F2, /n, /o, setting up Area Menus & User Parameters.
- Training will be one-to-one and classroom training one to many; the nature of training will depend on special requirements. For example, difficulty with new document types set-up and need for more hands-on training could engineer consultant classroom training onsite.

<u>Level (2) - Training Review and Further Development:</u>

- This is the next level of training development and delivery; this level I call 'Training Review and Further Development'.
- This level of training will be dependent on the following enquiry:

  (i)   Set-up of Independent Assessment (probably using an Independent Assessor) to see where top-up training is needed, for example for Executives and Business Managers.

  (ii)   Where the needs are (which departments ?)

  (iii)   And where the procedures are not quite right.

  (iv)   And on the basis of Level (1) to Level (3), draw up and develop a training plan.

- At level 2, you have got to get business benefits and payback from the system design, data set-up and implementation. Hence, you begin to train Executives and Business Managers how to get their key figures out on customers, materials, vendors, suppliers, orders, stock transfers (within and between storage locations, plants and warehouses), stock movements (goods issues, goods receipt and inventory adjustments), stocks lists and profitability and to derive business benefits from the data using standard SAP tools such as ABAP Query, Logistic/ Purchasing/ Sales Information System (i.e. creation of new info structures, P/SIS Rebuild), Pricing Reports and Analysis, New Outputs, VAT Account Determination, setting up key fields in Customer/ Material master data, Foreign Trade, selection of relevant Reports and programs using ABAP/4 Workbench, Program Amendments, System Upgrade etc.
- Training on new things - typical night follow day stuff.

<u>Stage (3) - Training Heights and Depth:</u>

The third level is what I call 'Training Heights and Depth'. If the continuous arrows on the boarders of the box give any indication, the height and depth of training (of continous training) can not be determined nor estimated. Hence, for a successful user training, system design, data set-up and implementation, the answer is 'more training and more training and more training and more training'. This will ultimately result in continuous innovation.

- The height and depth of training is influenced by excellent conditions of training. For example, availability of quality trainers and delivery; excellent classroom facilities; right attitudes of trainees, program planners, assessors and change managers; and constant review of training plans and development.
- If it is true that the core or centre of the box is a reflection of the whole box, level 1 (train the key business users and project management team from basic settings to complex configurations depending on work tasks and security

authorizations) is the core of the success of consultant, project team, user training and development; level 2 (Training Review and Further Development) builds upon level 1. Conditions of training enhance the quality of training development and delivery.

. Overall success and smooth running of training is dependent on the ability to provide quality training for all categories of users who seek it and need it within the project team and business, and for them to enjoy the experience of learning SAP R/3, even if they have never enjoyed any form of learning in the past.

. I am also particularly interested in how training could also benefit Business Development Executives, Accountants and Auditors, Supply Chain Managers, Corporate Financiers (Investment Bankers), Legal Specialists involved in Mergers and Acquisitions and SAP R/3 legal validation, and other specialists and professionals also, directly and indirectly, involved in cross border and transnational transactions and those areas that conglomerates cut across.

X.III   Lessons from the Conglomerates and Transborder Corporations

The strength and growth of a lot of complex conglomerates and transborder corporations from one generation to the next rest in the three key abilities stated above and further summarised here: (i) training employees on work tasks; (ii) continuous training review and further development (that is, continuous research); and (iii) continuous depth and innovation regarding the goods and services they create and provide to their markets. This is essentially the standard basis of their continuous training.

Chapter Eleven: Benefits of SAP R/3

XI.I Generation of Reports (ABAP Queries and BI gives the added value across modules)

The possibilities of generating all types of reports from standard SAP R/3 lists, ABAP queries and Business Intelligence Warehouse gives added value to the generation of reports across various SAP R/3 modules.

IX.II Seamless integration of various areas of the business into integrated whole (SD, MM, FI, COPA, PM, CRM, PP, SM / CS)

The seamless integration of various areas of a business into an integrated whole today seemed almost impossible a few decades ago. This is the magic of seamless integration of various SAP R/3 modules (such as Sales and Distribution, Materials Management, Financial Accounting, Controlling and Profitability Accounting, Industry Solution – Oil and Gas, Plant Maintenance, Customer Relationship Management, Production Planning, Service Management also known as Customer Service).

It makes it much easier managing different businesses and increases accountability and efficiencies.

IX.III Seamless integration of SAP R/3 with third party softwares

Seamless integration of SAP R/3 with third party softwares such as Servicemax, Clarify, Mobile Solution, CRM, BI, Adobe Flex.

XI.IV   Unique programming language ABAP

A unique programming language ABAP is used to create the system programs, reports, documents, transactions and various modules. An SAP R/3 is well grounded.

XI.V Most of the Forbes 500 global corporations run SAP R/3

Most of the Forbes 500 global corporations run SAP R/3, hence you will be building your hands-on skill and professional career on excellent software.

XI.VI   Lessons from the Conglomerates and Transborder Corporations

SAP R/3 makes much easier running complex and diverse organisations, and goods and services across boundaries, in an integrated way.

SAP R/3 and Mergers and Acquisitions (M&A of corporations having SAP R/3 as the core systems would give plausible leverage advantages, and what financiers and lawyers should know about Business Systems Evaluation and Synergy pre and post Acquisitions)

The prologue gave a narration of systems application and conglomerates (the challenges to seamless business process information technology for medium to large scale conglomerates and transborder corporations). We posit that today, SAP R/3 is at the core of many systems applications that many conglomerates and transborder will use to maintain their business process expertise. We also posit that today, mergers and acquisition are at the heart of growth strategy and synergy achievement in many conglomerates and transborder corporations. As many M&A are believed to fail, it therefore becomes important to see how successful systems applications with SAP R/3 at the core of growth strategy and synergy achievement could bring about plausible leverage advantages in achieving a successful M&A.

Mergers and Acquisitions (M&A) of corporations having SAP R/3 as their core systems would give plausible leverage advantages to businesses coming together either through mergers or acquisitions. For this to occur: *'Business Systems Evaluation and Synergy' should be at the core of successful M&A dealmaking.* Whilst much progress has been made in the area of application of best information technology best practices to businesses, particularly cross country and across boundary organisations, there is also need for responsible actions by M&A lawyers, investment bankers and advisers. There are just so many financiers and lawyers who do not know about *Business Systems Evaluation and Synergy*, which should be at the core of their dealmaking. The fact that the financial figures of bringing organisations together works fine on paper is never the actual reality when the M&A transactions are completed.

Many times when M&A dealmakers complete their transactions, consultants and project managers inherit both the good, bad and ugly decisions in bringing these businesses together, from an IT and ERP applications perspective. At times I wondered why certain organisations were acquired or merged with another when there seemed to be little or no business systems synergy between the acquirer and the acquired business. Dissatisfaction among employees and customers are always extensive, and the boomerangs always cause sleepless nights for all, including the company executives who made and sponsored the M&A decision in the first place. It is also at this time that both the financiers and lawyers are out of the picture and have moved on to other deals.

What Financiers and Lawyers should know concerning Business Systems Evaluation and Synergy:

(i)   For medium and large scale M&A, operating synergy of systems should be at the core of deal decision making;

(ii)   Or else business systems staff dissatisfaction and loss of relationship management between the acquirer and the business acquired business systems staff when synergies do not exist.

(iii)   When business systems synergy exist, extra cost on business systems design, data set-up and global implementations and jet-set consulting are reduced, because business synergy already exists between the acquirer and the acquired business.

(iv)   Time loss in discussions to achieve synergy after mergers and acquisitions are reduced.

(v)   When synergies already exist, loss of profit as a consequence of merging or acquiring new businesses are minimised.

(vi)   Eventual business loss and sale due to non-synergy of the acquirer and the acquired business are reduced.

(vii)   *Business Systems Evaluation and Synergy* can be achieved with SAP R/3, particularly when the acquirer and the acquired business(es) use SAP R/3 as their core systems. Hence synergy is much easier to achieve.

(viii)   Financiers and lawyers could carry out basic business system evaluation analysis asking such synergy questions such as: (a) Analysis of systems in place and core systems in the companies of interest for M&A; (b) Analyse the ability to streamline and synergise the business systems of the acquirer and the acquired business; (c) At what cost? How much is required for system alignment between the acquirer and the acquired business during negotiations of purchase and not after; (d) Will existing core business systems between the acquirer and the acquired business achieve business systems cost savings?

Business system synergy and alignment should be at the core of M&A financing (investment banking) and due diligence (handled by lawyers). Using SAP R/3 as leverage for business operational excellence between similar organisations is a wise thing to do to achieve a successful M&A.

Good business synergy judgements and decisions by business leaders, M&A corporate financiers and lawyers make much easier the professional work of SAP R/3 consultants that need to bring merged or acquired businesses together.

Checklists for Business Systems Evaluation and Synergy for Mergers and Acquisitions

I. General Information on IT Infrastructure of the Acquirer

(1)   How many countries covered by the Conglomerate and Transborder Corporation?

(2)   How many sites in each country?

(3)   How many PC users in each site?

(4)   How many PC users globally?

(5)   Complexity and sophistication of IT infrastructure?

(6)   Is IT maintained centrally or separately in each country and site?

(7)   What is the primary software for process management, financial accounting and control in the conglomerate and transborder corporation? Is it SAP R/3, Oracle, Peoplesoft, Baan, J D Edwards or a mixture or in-house developed system?

(8)   What are the secondary (third party) systems interfaced to the primary IT system?

(9)   Does the Acquirer Conglomerate and Transborder have the necessary resources, both human capital, funds and project experience to bring in new companies into the Acquirers Conglomerate and Transborder business?

(10) Is synergy of IT systems part of due diligence and what is the weight of importance in the Mergers and Acquisition decision?

(11) What percentage when compared to Corporate Finance and Legal Advisory in any acquisition?

(12) IT Infrastructure and Competence Centre costs of the Conglomerate and Transborder Corporation, what is the percentage of revenue? Acquiring another organisation, will over all percentage reduce? Reduction preferred.

(13) IT Infrastructure and Competence Centre costs of the Conglomerate and Transborder Corporation, what is the percentage of expenditure? Acquiring another organisation, will overall percentage reduce or increase? Reduction preferred.

(14) IT Infrastructure and Competence Centre cost of the Conglomerate and Transborder Corporation, what is the percentage of profit? Reduction preferred.

II. General Information on IT Infrastructure of the Acquired organisation

(15) How many countries covered by the Acquired Conglomerate and Transborder Corporation and what are the similarities and differences with the Acquirer organisation?

(16) How many sites in each country and what are the similarities and differences with the Acquirer organisation?

(17) How many PC users in each site compared with the Acquirer organisation? Will this increase IT cost of Acquirer and by how much? How much leverage in the medium term and long term?

(18) How many PC users globally compared with the Acquirer organisation? Will this increase IT cost of Acquirer and by how much? How much leverage in the medium term and long term?

(19) Complexity and sophistication of IT infrastructure? Will this increase IT cost of Acquirer and by how much? How much leverage in the medium term and long term?

(20) Is IT maintained centrally or separately in each country and site? What will be the benefits of IT maintained centrally compared to diversified and independent IT sites and networks to the acquiring organisation?

(21) What is the primary software for process management, financial accounting and control in the acquired organisation ? Is it SAP R/3, Oracle, Peoplesoft, Baan, J D Edwards or a mixture or in-house developed system?

(22) IS THERE ANY SYNERGY WITH ACQUIRING ORGANIATSION PRIMARY SOFTWARE? An SAP R/3 SYNERGY PREFERRED.

(23) What are the secondary (third party) systems interfaced to the primary IT system? Is there any synergy with acquiring organisation secondary softwares? Synergy preferred.

(24) Does the Acquired Conglomerate and Transborder have **WILLING** human capital and project experience to work cooperatively with the Acquirers Conglomerate and Transborder business for a unified mission?

(25) Is synergy of IT systems part of due diligence and what is the weight of importance in the Mergers and Acquisition decision? What percentage when compared to Corporate Finance and Legal Advisory in the sale of the business?

(26) IT Infrastructure and Competence Centre costs of the acquired organisation, what is the percentage of revenue? Selling to another organisation, will overall percentage reduce? Reduction preferred.

(27) IT Infrastructure and Competence Centre costs of the acquired organisation, what is the percentage of expenditure? Selling to another organisation, will overall percentage reduce or increase? Reduction preferred.

(28) IT Infrastructure and Competence Centre cost of the acquired organisation, what will be the percentage of profit of the acquiring organisation in the medium and long term? Reduction preferred.

III. Business Systems Evaluation and Synergy for Mergers and Acquisitions

(29) For medium and large scale M&A, operating synergy of systems should be at the core of deal decision-making. Is this the case with this mergers and acquisition from an IT perspective?

(30) Or else business systems staff dissatisfaction and loss of relationship management between the acquirer and the business acquired business systems staff when synergies do not exist. Is this the case with this mergers and acquisition from an IT perspective?

(31) When business systems synergy exist, extra cost on business systems design, data set-up and global implementations and jet-set consulting are reduced, because business synergy already exists between the acquirer and the acquired business. Is this the case with this mergers and acquisition from an IT perspective?

(32) Time loss in discussions to achieve synergy after mergers and acquisition is reduced. Is this the case with this mergers and acquisition from an IT perspective?

(33) When synergies already exist, loss of profit as a consequence of merging or acquiring new businesses is minimised. Is this the case with this mergers and acquisition from an IT perspective?

(34) Eventual business loss and sale due to non-synergy of the acquirer and the acquired business are reduced. Is this the case with this mergers and acquisition from an IT perspective?

(35) *Business Systems Evaluation and Synergy* can be achieved with SAP R/3, particularly when the acquirer and the acquired business(es) use SAP R/3 as their core systems. Hence synergy is much easier to achieve. Is this the case with this mergers and acquisition from an IT perspective?

(36) Financiers and lawyers could carry out basic business system evaluation analysis asking such synergy questions such as: (a) Analysis of systems in place and core systems in the companies of interest for M&A; (b) Analyse the ability to streamline and synergise the business systems of the acquirer and the acquired business; (c) At what cost? How much is required for system alignment between the acquirer and the acquired business during negotiations of purchase and not after; (d) Will existing core business systems between the acquirer and the acquired business achieve business systems cost savings? Is this the case with this mergers and acquisition from an IT perspective?

These *Checklists for Business Systems Evaluation and Synergy for Mergers and Acquisitions* should be helpful in any successful M&A due diligence from an IT competency perspective (pre and post acquisition management, disruptions and costs) and hence should minimise failure and dissatisfaction. The probability of successful M&A is increased.

Conclusion

For non-SAP R/3 professionals, an SAP R/3 system should be of serious concern to Mergers and Acquisition Corporate Financiers (investment bankers), M&A legal advisers and those professionals who from time to time are involved in decision-making concerning mergers, acquisitions and dispositions of corporate and project assets in conglomerates and transborder corporations that uses SAP R/3 as their core ERP software. This handbook gives you a short synopsis of what you should know and why concerning SAP R/3, and should influence your pre and post acquisition investment analysis and due diligence.

For SAP R/3 consultants, I hope you will be able to survive your early beginnings in an SAP environment with this succinct information, and thereafter move on to expertise and excellence in your career. Many years experience is now summarised in a few pages and a few hours of learning for you to become established in your career. If so, one of the objectives of this short synopsis of SAP R/3 has been achieved.

This book, using the Sales and Distribution module as a case study, is useful for all SAP R/3 functional and technical consultants in the early stages of their career. The same design, configuration and SAP R/3 technical methodology that applies to the Sales and Distribution module also applies to other SAP R/3 modules. SAP R/3 methodology is a systematically organised top down step-by-step methodology using the ABAP programming language.

This SAP R/3 book does not make you a qualified and certified SAP R/3 consultant. It is important you attend an *SAP Academy* to get properly trained and certified, in specific areas you are interested in. SAP training offices are available in many countries now around the world.

This book especially builds your understanding and confidence, and helps in defining in a structured manner what is expected of you, in terms of general knowledge, in an SAP R/3 environment in one working day, without getting embarrassed and unnecessarily fearful, particularly if and when you find yourself working for one of the conglomerates and transborder corporations.

In conglomerates and transborder corporations you may have to specialise and become expert in specific area(s) of this handbook. In small businesses that have or will implement SAP R/3, you will have to know much more and in detail.

Reiterating, for those corporate executives, M&A specialists, investment bankers and lawyers that will also peruse this book, it will be very beneficial in their decision making concerning pre and post acquisition management (including IT / ERP disruptions and costs) and hence should minimise failure and dissatisfaction. The probability of successful M&A is increased in conglomerates and transborder corporations.

Bibliography

Administering SAP R/3: SD - Sales and Distribution Module. Que Corporation 1999.